African Violets

Also by Melvin J. Robey

Home Lawn Care
Lawns

African Violets

Queens of the Indoor Gardening Kingdom

Melvin J. Robey

Illustrated by Nanci P. Robey

SAN DIEGO • NEW YORK
A. S. BARNES & COMPANY, INC.
IN LONDON:
THE TANTIVY PRESS

The Tantivy Press
Magdalen House
136-148 Tooley Street
London, SE1 2TT, England
First Edition
Manufactured in the United States of America
For information write to A. S. Barnes and Company, Inc.,
P.O. Box 3051, San Diego, CA 92038

Library of Congress Cataloging in Publication Data

Robey, Melvin J
  African violets, queens of the indoor gardening kingdom.

  Includes index.
  1.   African violets.   I.   Title.
SB413.A4R63   635.9'33'81   78-75332
ISBN 0-498-02349-4

1 2 3 4 5 6 7 8 9 84 83 82 81 80

All color photographs are courtesy of the African
Violet Society of America, unless noted otherwise in
the captions.

Contents

African Violets

1
African Violets: A Gift from Nature

*I*n 1865 Dr. David Livingston was actively engaged in his pursuit of becoming the first European to find the origin of the Nile River. After several years of searching the African continent he finally discovered Lake Victoria as the source of the world's greatest river. This great lake is bordered on the east side by Tanzania and Kenya with their desert lands and high mountain ranges. Had Dr. Livingtone taken the time and interest in the flora of the area he surely would have been credited as being the discoverer of African violets.

Baron Walter von Saint Paul is credited as being the first person to realize the importance of the little purple flowering plants growing among the foothills and peaks of the Usambara Mountains. In the late 1800s, while serving as Governor of East German Africa, he collected several plants in the northern area of Tanzania. On seeing these plants for the first time he knew he had found a plant of horticultural value. He was confident that with some research and breeding work a new and beautiful flowering plant would be available to flower lovers around the world.

In 1892, Baron von Saint Paul sent seed from these plants to his father, Baron Ulrich von Saint Paul of Fischback-Silesia, Germany. The elder von Paul took an immediate interest in the new variety of flowers sent to him. After growing the plants from seed and observing the delicate flowers he shared the discovery with his friends, who were members of the Royal Botanic Gardens of Germany. It wasn't until a taxonomist, Hermann Wendland, director of the Royal Botanic Gardens, studied the individual characteristics of this unusual plant and concluded that an entirely new species had been discovered.

In one year's time the new plants captured the attention of horticulturists all over Europe. During the 1893 International Horticulture Show, African violet plants shared the spotlight with another exotic plant—the orchid. Both plants shared the distinction of being named the most exciting plants at the show. The first botanical description of these new plants appeared in the German magazine, *Gartenflora*, in 1893, introducing the plant to everyone who did not see it at the international flower show.

Plant breeders at once began to develop new and improved varieties. Interest was primarily in developing different colored flowers and seeing whether the size of the flowers could be increased. In a very short time African violets were available in a multitude of blossom colors: pink, white, wine-colored, many shades of blue, and purple and red. Eager plant explorers have searched the world over for new varieties, but it is through the dedication of the plant breeders that there are so many beautiful varieties of African violets.

To better understand your African violets, a trip to East Africa would be an enjoyable excursion. Once there, you could walk along the footpaths of the Usambara Mountains and gaze at a wide variety of African violets. If you don't think such a trip is in your future, the following geographic information will help paint a picture of the climate and landscape in which the African violets thrive. From this information you'll have a better understanding of the cultural requirements of these plants.

African violets are indigenous to the Usambara Mountains located 100 miles from the east coast of Africa. These mountains reach 8,800 to 9,000 feet above sea level and extend for 75 to 80 miles. African violets can be found clinging to life in the cracks and crevices of shear rock cliffs as high as 6,500 feet. At the lower elevation in the lush tropical valleys the delicate plants can be found growing more abundantly.

The temperature and humidity are always very high wherever African violets are found thriving in nature. Temperatures in the mid to upper eighties are not unusual, with the humidity at 90 to 95 percent. Very little fluctuation between day and night temperatures has allowed the plants to adapt to living in a fairly constant temperature. Because of this unique adaptation the African violets have learned to grow and produce flowers year round, never needing to go into a four-to-eight-week dormant resting period. This is one of the primary reasons why African violets are such a popular houseplant. There is nothing more delightful in a home than an African violet plant in full bloom on a cold winter's day when there's a foot or two of snow outside covering up the lawn and flowerbeds.

Twenty-seven different species of African violets have been given names, all of which are native to the African Continent. Two other possible species exist but are not yet classified as true species. Differences between most of these species are not easy to distinguish. In most instances you would have to be an expert to be able to separate one species from another.

Many beautiful tropical plants in the world are closely related to African violets. One tiny relative found growing in South American barely reaches two inches in height at full maturity. And another distant relative from a Pacific island is several feet tall. Some of the better known relatives are: gloxinia, streptocarpus, columnea, sinningia, episcia, and achimenes.

ORIGIN OF AFRICAN VIOLETS

African violets were discovered growing wild in the foothills of the Usambara Mountains. In less than 100 years these majestic plants have become the favorite indoor flowering plant throughout the world.

Americans Discover African Violets

Early records place the first African violets as arriving in the United States somewhere around 1894, just one scant year after their introduction in Europe. W. K. Harris, a Philadelphia florist, obtained plants from a New York shop that had just received a shipment of the new plants. By the early 1900s some African violets finally found their way into a few homes. The popularity of the little plants lagged for many years because very little was known about them or the care they needed. Lack of flowers and sickly looking foliage destined these early plants to the garbage or compost heaps.

It was left up to the enterprising plant breeders to develop the new varieties homeowners would accept and be able to grow successfully. A West Coast plant nursery undertook this task in 1927. Seeds from England and Germany were ordered by the Armacost and Royston Nursery in the Los Angeles area. From these seeds approximately 1,000 African violet plants were grown for use in developing new, improved varieties. It is from this humble beginning that the present wave of interest in growing African violets got its start.

Out of these 1,000 plants ten were selected as the best, exhibiting those characteristics most desirable by plant growers and home gardeners. Features such as the appearance of nice green foliage, profuse flowering, and flower color were important criteria in the selection process. All the flowers were blue, purple, violet, or a variation of these colors.

Two of the ten selected plants came from the German seed and were given the names "Blue Boy" and "Sailor Boy." The other eight plants were from the English seed and were called Admiral, Amethyst, Commodore, Mermaid, Neptune, Norseman, Number 32, and Viking.

Hybridization of these plants has given African violet hobbyists literally hundreds of different varieties from which to choose. With the help of an excellent breeding program and watchful readiness for any mutant (sometimes called sports) characteristics that could be bred into the African violets, many different types were developed. African violets with ruffled leaf edges, flowers of varying shapes (star and buttercup), leaf color variance, flowering color from soft to deep purples, multicolored flowers, and flowers with an increased number of petals (doubles and semidoubles) were developed.

Plant breeders were also busy working on the development of African violets with differences in their growing habits. Miniature plants were developed that were exact replicas of the normal-sized African violets. Perfect in every feature, these miniatures are delicate-looking plants that will enhance any location in the house. They are an excellent choice for African violet hobbyists who have limited space to devote to their hobby.

What's in a Name?

After a plant is discovered and has gone through a painstaking examination to determine whether it is indeed a new species, it must be given a scientific name. The Director of the Botanical Gardens honored the father and son who had introduced this fascinating plant to the world by naming it after them. He called it *Saintpaulia ionantha.* The second part of the name refers to the flowers as appearing like true violets. Wendland in his early writings continued to compare the new plants with the violets familiar to him. He gave the plants the common name of Usambara Vielchen, after the violets and mountains where the plants were first found growing.

12

African violets and true violets are often confused by gardeners as being the same plant. Each one is entirely different and can easily be distinguished from the other one. Use the characteristics shown here to properly identify these two plants.

TRUE VIOLET

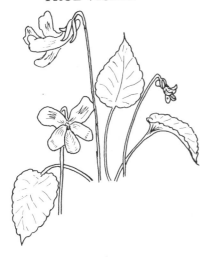

—Flowers consist of five petals with the lower one rolled up into a structure referred to as a spur.
—Each flower has five stamens with the lower two projecting into the blossom spur.
—The solitary flowers rise up from the plant on a long peduncle.
—Some species in this group produce yellow flowers.
—Mature seed pods consist of three distinct cells or capsules.

AFRICAN VIOLET

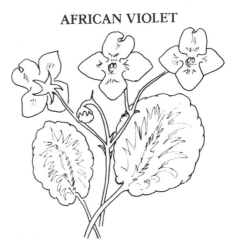

—Usually a plant has two stamens: may have more in plants with double blossoms.
—Flower has five petals; none form a spur-like structure.
—Numerous flowers borne in clusters on a single peduncle.
—No known species has produced a yellow flower.
—Mature seed pods composed of a single cell or capsule.

Eventually the name was changed by the English to African violets because it is easier to pronounce. Calling these plants ''violets'' is very misleading because African violets are not even closely related to true violets. Although the flowers may look somewhat alike, the plants belong in an entirely different family. True violets belong to the Violaceae Family and are found growing in the wild throughout the United States. The African violet is a member of the Gesneriaceae Family and for the most part is grown only indoors.

An easy way to distinguish a true violet from an African violet is by careful examination of the flowers. One characteristic feature of a true violet is the fusing of one petal on each flower into a tubular or rolled-like petal called a spur. African violet flowers do not form spurs on any known species.

Let's tackle the scientific names of the African violets and learn how to pronounce them. Latin names often inhibit gardeners and create a mental block whereby they never bother to learn them. You can always turn heads at any party if in the normal conversation of discussing your African violets you can slip in the Latin names. Your friends will label you as a true enthusiast and eventually spread the word around that you are an expert on African violets.

First, let's look at the breakdown of the family name Gesneriaceae—ges-neer-ee-ay'-see-ee. Try it a few times until it rolls off your tongue easily. Next, try the scientific name (genus and species) *Saintpaulia ionantha*—saint-paul'-ee-a eye-o-nan'-tha. Try to be as accurate as possible; an acquaintance may have also read this book.

Popularity of African Violets Soars

There are many reasons why African violets have become everyone's favorite indoor flowering plant. Almost every household has at least one plant tucked away somewhere, creating a splash of beauty for the beholder to enjoy year round. It is the one household plant that always flowers, trying to cheer you up regardless of the weather out-of-doors.

What has led to the poplarity of African violets? An answer to this question will require taking a look at many different features which make these plants a favorite. Totaling all the attributes of the African violets will give you an excellent idea of how one plant species could raise itself high above the others and proudly stand as the Queen of the Indoor Gardening Kingdom.

Numerous new varieties, plus the old standards, provide a wide range of African violets from which homeowners can select their plants. Features such as flower color, leaf shape, and size of the plant all allow people to pick and choose plants according to their own individual tastes.

The ease with which African violets can be propagated strongly figures in their popularity. Exchanging leaf cuttings is common practice among African violet hobbyists. Everyone enjoys giving a gift to a friend, and what better gift is there than a living plant you have nursed from a cutting to a beautiful flowering African violet. Your friends will be greatly impressed by your expertise and very appreciative of the thoughtful gift.

Very little space is needed for growing African violets—a windowsill, a corner on a bookshelf, or tucked away on a decorative shelf in the bathroom; all are excellent spots to display these lovely little plants. The cost of buying African violets is very nominal and they can be obtained at almost any garden center, nursery, or the larger department store. And, again, the ease of propagating African violets allows them to be increased at practically no cost.

African violets can be grown under a wide range of growing conditions. Fortunately the temperature and humidity requirements of these plants are very similar to those you enjoy in your home, making them very compatible to your lifestyle.

African violets tucked away in a bookcase give a room a touch of elegance. Hidden fluorescent lights will allow the plants to bloom year round for your enjoyment. *Courtesy of Duro-Lite Lamps, Inc.*

When buying an African violet from a greenhouse or florist shop, you must remember that these plants are growing in a controlled climate. Everything is perfect for a beautiful plant to develop and look its best when sold to a customer.

What happens to these same plants when you take them home? They are absolutely beautiful for a few weeks, then something goes wrong. The plants seem to lose their vigor, leaves may even drop off, and flowers begin to fade, wilt, and fall off too. But don't panic! This is just a passing phase your new African violets are going through. After being grown under ideal conditions in a greenhouse, you have moved them to a location in your home with an entirely new environment. African violets display great ability to adjust to new living conditions, and in a very short time will return to their former majestic stature. This may require from two to four weeks.

Both the expert and the novice can enjoy working with African violets and find growing them a very satisfying hobby. An experienced grower can have beautiful plants with very little work by following a few simple rules on their care.

All these unique features of African violets combine to create plants that will make it easier for every homeowner to be a successful gardener. In our present ''green-thumb'' society nearly everyone wants to be able to identify with some phase of gardening. African violets fill this need for many people because they need only simple care to produce beautiful flowering plants.

Tips on Buying Your African Violets

Going to the greenhouse or nursery store to buy a few African violets for your home or as gifts is a very nice way to spend an afternoon. It is always enjoyable to walk through the aisles of a greenhouse and observe all the different plants, many of which come from the far corners of the earth. The wide range of shapes and colors the different varieties display is breathtaking. Thoroughly enjoy your visit while gazing at all the exotic plants; but when it is time to pick out your African violets, it will help if you keep a couple of facts in mind:

Always look for a plant in a small pot, preferably a clay pot. Smaller plants will adapt more quickly to the environment in your home. Do not plan to repot an African violet until it has been growing in your home for at least one month. Remember that you are taking the plant from perfect growing conditions and moving it into an entirely different situation in which it will need time to adjust.

Look over the foliage very carefully. There should be no blemishes on the leaves, and the absence of any insects or disease should be noted. Check the leaf arrangement by looking directly down on top of the plant. Does the rosette of leaves have good symmetry? By this I mean are the leaves of the plant distributed evenly around the plant. This is important if an African violet is to become a showpiece in your home. To maintain this symmetry you will have to rotate the plant one-quarter of a turn several times each week so all parts of it are exposed an equal amount of time to the sunshine.

Welcome to the world of African violets!

Whether you are just starting out with your first plant, or can be regarded as an avid African violet hobbyist, the fun and excitement of growing these superbly flowering plants are immeasurable. How else can you spend a few relaxing minutes or hours each day seeing to the needs of some living thing and be so richly rewarded for your endeavors?

2
Botany and Other Facts

African violets are truly fascinating plants. They have a multitude of looks for the African violet hobbyist to admire—from plain leaf varieties with simple beautiful flowers, to those with heavily rippled leaf edges and large double blossoms. The beauty of these plants is indisputable when they have the proper care to allow them to reach a peak of perfection. Specific information on how to care for African violets is not included here but is covered in the remaining chapters.

The purpose of this chapter is to introduce you to the numerous features and characteristics displayed by African violet plants. So when you read or hear someone talking about a ''girl plant'' or a Geneva-type blossom, you will know what is being described to you. You'll also learn about such things as how to develop new varieties of African violets through hybridization and the classification of the leaves according to the shape of their margins (leaf edges). Flower colors, varieties of African violets available from which you can choose, and many other interesting tidbits will be touched on for your use in developing a better understanding of this plant.

Have you ever worked with your African violets and wondered why some flowers are all one color and others may display several colors? Has a friend ever asked you if any of your plants are ''sports?'' Do you know why the leaves of some African violets have smooth edges and others are ruffled? When you are spending your spare time with your plants, wouldn't it be fun to know the answers to questions like these? One of the real joys of growing African violets is understanding how they grow and being able to identify the distinctive features that add so much to the appearance of each plant.

As an African violet hobbyist you needn't be swamped with a great deal of scientific information on things such as the Kreb Cycle, meiosis, phosphorylases, or Liebig's theory. And don't worry about it, because I'm leaving these areas to the scientists who are paid to work in a laboratory eight hours a day. My objective is to expose you to the world of African violets so you will have the necessary credentials to proceed toward becoming a master gardener of African violets.

AFRICAN VIOLETS COME IN A VARIETY OF SIZES

LARGE

Greater than 16″ diameter

STANDARD

8″ to 16″ diameter

MINIATURE

less than a 6″ diameter

SEMI-MINIATURE

6″ to 8″ diameter

This scale drawing allows you to compare the sizes of the different classifications of African violet plants.

19

Description of African Violets

African violets come in a wide assortment of sizes; some are as small as four inches across, and others easily reach twenty or more inches in diameter. For convenience, four classes of African violets have been designated. Miniature African violets are the tiny ones, six inches or less in diameter. The semiminiatures vary from six to eight inches at maturity, and the standard plants range from eight to sixteen inches in diameter. African violets placed in the very largest classification have a diameter of over sixteen inches and may become so large they will barely fit through a house door. In the homes of some avid African violet growers plants in this last group have measured thirty-eight to forty inches.

Anatomy of an African Violet

Let's look at an individual plant and discuss the numerous botanical features that make the plant so attractive. The individual leaves rise from the base of the plant, grow out over the pot, and form a rosette of leaves. The leaf margins come in a wide assortment of shapes and range from being smooth to having ruffled, fluted, or wavy edges. The tip of each plant leaf

BOTANY OF THE AFRICAN VIOLET PLANT

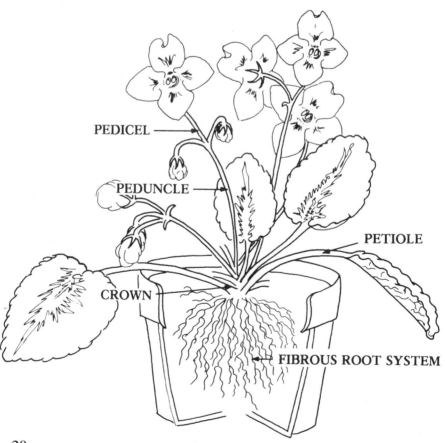

PEDICEL

PEDUNCLE

PETIOLE

CROWN

FIBROUS ROOT SYSTEM

may be either pointed or rounded, with the leaf base (stem end of the leaf) often being heart-shaped. Hairy-like appendages are usually, but not always, found growing from the surface of most of the leaves. The fuzzy leaves are especially beautiful in the light, which causes the leaves to take on a silvery appearance.

Blossoms originate from the crown of the African violet plant. In the early stages of development a flower and leaf bud are difficult to distinguish; so if you are disbudding flowers, be sure to wait until you are positive of the identity of the developing structure. The flower bud stalk will be curled up, and as it grows it unwinds and reaches through the rosette of leaves toward the light.

The stalk bearing the flower is called a peduncle. Anywhere from two to ten blossoms will be borne from each peduncle. The flower petals (collectively called the corolla) come in a variety of colors.

The flower formed by the five individual petals is beautiful and unique. Outside of the African violet family no other plant species in the world has a flower exactly like it. The petals are divided into two separate parts called lips. The upper lip consists of two petals and the lower lip has three petals. The upper lip's petals are smaller; the three lower petals are much larger and are more readily identifiable because they stand out as individual petals. The upper lip's petals appear almost as a single unit, if you are not familiar with the flowers of an African violet. The petals all fuse together around the stamens and pistil, forming a tubular collar which then extends down to the base of the flower where the petals are attached to the pedicel.

Each flower contains both male and female reproductive organs. The bright-yellow appendages seen in the center of each flower are the male parts called stamens. Inside these structures is where the pollen is produced. The female part of the flower, known as the pistil, receives the pollen and is located alongside the stamens. The pistil extends above the stamens and looks like a thread sticking up from the center of the flower.

Read over the description of the plant and flowers two or three times, and study the illustrations to form a picture in your mind of all the various parts of an African violet. After you master all the terminology and know each plant part, spend some time studying an Africal violet plant. Without looking at the illustrations try to identify as many parts of the plant as you can remember.

Remove a blossom or two from one of your plants and dissect it. To do this, fold all five petals together so the tips of each are touching and gently pull until they come free as a single unit. This will leave the pistil exposed so you can readily see the various parts. The five green appendages on which the pistil is sitting are sepals (collectively known as the calyx). Next, use a sharp razor blade and slice through the center of the yellow stamens. Tap the stamens on your thumb, and you'll see a small cloud of the dustlike pollen escaping.

If any of this pollen were to land on the pistil of a plant fertilization would occur, and the new seeds would begin to grow in the ovary of the plant. The number of black and brown seeds per pod (dried ovary) will vary from 400 to

THE ANATOMY OF THE AFRICAN VIOLET FLOWER

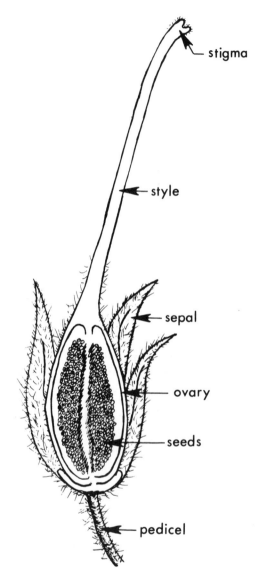

The female part of the flower is called the pistil, which is composed of three parts: the stigma, a style, and an ovary.

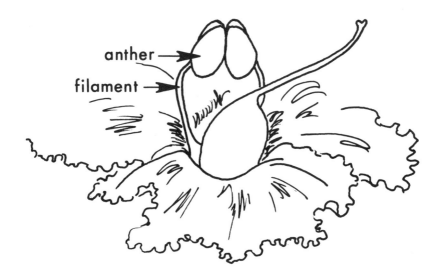

anther

filament

The male parts of the flower are known as the stamens and consist of two structures, the filaments and the anthers. This drawing shows the relationship between the stamens and the pistil on an African violet flower.

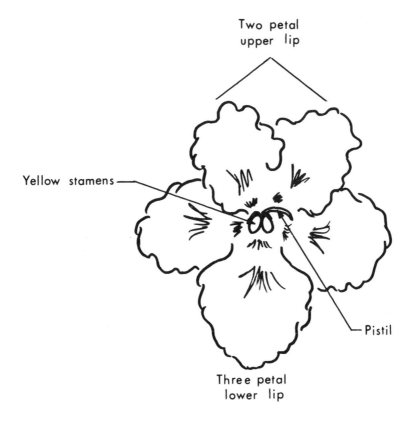

Two petal
upper lip

Yellow stamens

Pistil

Three petal
lower lip

The individual flower has three distinct features that attracts attention to their natural beauty—the stamens, the pistil, and the flower petals.

600. African violets that have white blossoms do not produce seed as easily as those with other blossom colors.

The seed is very small. Breathing on it is enough to scatter it all over. Someone once took the time to count the number of African violet seeds in an ounce. I don't know how long it took, but with 750,000 seeds per ounce I'm sure it was a tedious task.

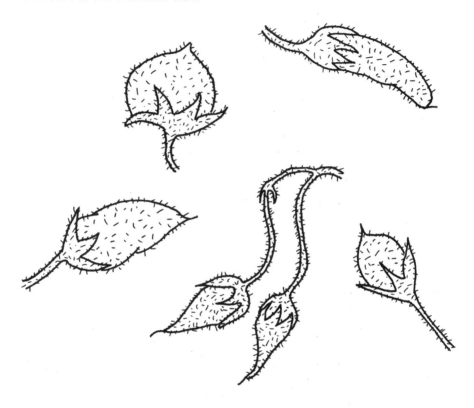

Maturing African violet seed pods may be seen in a variety of shapes and sizes. Each pod may contain 400 to 600 seeds.

Beware of Suckers

Often an African violet will send up a new shoot from the crown (base of the plant). A close inspection will show that it is growing in the axil of a leaf. These new plant shoots are referred to as "suckers" and develop into individual plants with their own crown. If left alone they will continue to grow and produce flowers just as the rest of the plant is doing. This is how a multicrowned African violet develops.

Should you wish to keep your African violet plants small, symmetrical, and looking like a show plant, these suckers should not be left on the plants.

To avoid the problem, check your African violets frequently for the growth of any suckers. If you discover one, remove it with a pair of sharp long-nosed scissors or use a razor blade. Suckers are easily rooted, so if you are interested in having a new African violet in the house try your luck at propagation. Chapter 8 on propagation explains how to root suckers.

Leaving suckers on an African violet will cause the plant to become monstrous and overcrowd the pot in which it is growing. When this happens, the health of the plant deteriorates; it quits flowering and is no longer an attractive plant. Division of multicrowned plants is also discussed in Chapter 8. It is much easier to remove a young sucker than to wait and later cut the plants apart. The shock of the operation often spells disaster for the African violet which is treated so roughly.

Boy and Girl Type Plants

The terms ''boy'' and ''girl'' are often used when discussing African violets. Frequent use of these terms has mislead gardeners into believing that African violets are either male or female plants, when in fact most African violets have both the stamens (male) and pistils (female) present in every flower. The exception to this rule is the occasional lack of any stamens in African violets that produce double blossoms.

Then to what do these two misleading terms refer if it isn't the sex of the plants? The words boy and girl describe a difference in the coloration of African violet leaves. Boy-type leaves are plain and solid green. Girl-type leaves display a white to yellowish color at the base of the leaf where the stem is attached, and often they have ruffled leaf edges.

All the leaves of the ten original African violets were entirely green, without the slightest trace of other colors. One of the varieties, 'Blue Boy,' produced a mutation that had the white-to-yellowish discoloration at the base of the leaf. These unusual African violets were given the name 'Blue Girl.' It was only natural for the plain-leaf varieties to be called boy-type plants, and those showing the discoloration to be known as girl-type plants.

You should be aware of another term commonly used to describe a plant that has mutated and no longer looks exactly like its parents. When this happens, it is said to have ''sported.'' One of the best examples of a sport in the African violet family is the girl-type foliage just discussed.

Leaf Characteristics to Know

The importance of the leaf is well known to plant scientists. Its role in photosynthesis, transpiration, and other plant functions has been well documented. In this section we are not interested in these processes but rather in those features of the leaf that are aesthetically pleasing to us. Fortunately interested African violet growers have been able to develop new hybrids which display a wide assortment of different and unusual leaf characteristics.

Names used to describe the various types of leaf margins will tell you fairly well what to expect. If the terms scallop, ruffled, fringed, wavy, fluted or serrated are used, then the leaf edges will be irregular. Some may have deep lobes in them and may be wrinkled, and others have edges like the teeth of a saw. Shape is often told when you read the leaves as spooned, cupped, pointed, longifolia, holly, or ovate. A quilted leaf is one with a puckered or raised area with seams, reminding you of the handstitched quilt given to you by your grandmother.

Good color in the leaves adds to the beauty of African violets. Many varieties produce bright-green leaves so attractive that it is hard to imagine there could be any prettier ones. Yet the variegated leaves of 'Happy Harold,' 'Winter Grape,' 'Half & Half,' and 'Watercolor' are truly magnificent to behold. The green foliage, interlaced with white pigment, creates an interesting plant for African violet fanciers to display in their homes.

Many violets have a red coloring on the underneath side of leaves. This feature adds a nice splash of color to these plants and is caused by a combination of factors you can control. The amount of light and the temperature govern the intensity of the red pigments found in the leaf. Be sure to select plants that have a tendency to display this feature if you are interested in it.

Hairy-like appendages can be seen growing from the leaf. These projections are so numerous on some plants that the leaves appear to be covered with a very soft fuzz. All African violets do not have these hairy-like appendages. Some are almost totally free of them and are referred to as being smooth-leafed varieties. Although this may detract from the beauty of a plant it does offer certain advantages. Dust doesn't accumulate as easily on the surface of these smooth leaves, and the dirt is easy to wash or brush off. Also, if you spill a few drops of water on the leaves it is very easy to dry them off.

Variety Shown in African Violet Blossoms

Flowers are found growing in clusters, exhibiting a multitude of colors: blue, pink, rose, orchid, lavender, red, maroon, plum, burgundy, purple, violet, white, creamy, and blush. All the different colors displayed by blossoms are the result of pigments present in the petals. Yellow is one color that has not been discovered in the petals of any African violet plants. The color of the pigment will change slightly due to outside influences acting on the plant. Light, temperature, soil mixture, soil pH, plant food—all affect the color of pigments. For example, normal pink petals will become very red when ample supplies of nitrogen and phosphorous are available to the plant. This will account for some of the changes noticed in the blossom color of some African violets.

Blossoms come in all sorts of color combinations as well as solid colors. The spectacular coloring of some blossoms has caused them to be divided into special categories according to the color design displayed by individual flower petals.

26

Bicolored blossoms have two distinct colors present in each petal. These colors may be dispersed, or appear only along the edge of the petal. Another term, multicolored, has the same meaning as bicolored except that it includes all blossoms with two or more colors present in the petals. Many blossoms have two hues (shades) of the same color in their petals. An example of this would be a petal with a light tone (hue) of lavender and a darker tone of purple. These blossoms are called two-toned.

Geneva-type blossoms are multicolored with white along the edges of the petals. Only those African violets with this characteristic blossom can be classified in this group. Fantasy blossoms with irregular splotches or streaks of color on the petals are another type. Often the petals look as if someone had sprinkled paint on them. African violets show a lot of different color combinations in their blossoms. It is the beauty of each blossom and the ability of the plant to produce them year round which have helped to make the plant so popular.

The attractiveness of African violet plants was greatly enhanced when the shape of the petals began to take on new and exciting forms. Now, along with the wide variety of choice in the colors available, you have several different flower shapes from which to choose.

Blossoms of the first African violets had only five single petals, each one with an ovate (rounded) tip. These are classified as single blossoms and are often referred to as "standard" or "tailored" blossoms. A slight variation of the shape of individual petals gave rise to a whole new type of blossom. When the petal tips became pointed, the blossoms took on the appearance of a five-pointed star, and became known as star-shape blossoms. Each of the petals are the same size and equally spaced, making this blossom even more distinct from a single blossom with its three larger and two smaller petals.

Eventually other African violet plants were developed which had ten petals instead of the normal five. It was not difficult to name this new group of blossoms. Since there were twice as many petals, the blossoms became know as doubles. African violets with double blossoms are among the most beautiful plants in the world. Semidouble blossoms can easily be confused with a double unless you examine the number of petals present on the blossoms. If the petals number somewhere from six to nine, the blossom is a semidouble. Ten separate panels must be present for a blossom to fit into the double category.

Blossoms with irregularly shaped petal edges fit into two separate types—fringed and ruffled. When the edges of petals are barely rippled, the petals are said to be fringed. If they are extremely irregular, then the blossoms are ruffled.

Fragrance is a desirable feature most flowers possess. Unfortunately, African violets are among the plants which do not have a scent. It is really too bad that such a lovely plant does not have its own distinctive aroma, but perhaps that is why nature has seen fit to bestow colorful and uniquely shaped blossoms on the African violets. So far as anyone knows, the African violet has never had a fragrant flower in its ancestry. Both plant breeders and

African violet hobbyists would like to develop a new variety of plants that produce fragrant flowers, but the chances of such a breakthrough do not appear to be on the horizon.

African Violet Varieties

Baron Walter von Saint Paul did not realize that the plants he collected and sent to Germany were two different species within the same genus—*Saintpaulia*. Even the horticulturists at the Royal Botanical Gardens were unaware of the fact that the plants were indeed slightly different from one another. The original plants were all thought to be *Saintpaulia ionantha*, but later the second species was identified as *Saintpaulia confusa*. It is from these two individuals that most of the African violet plants can claim their heritage. It was a stroke of luck that the Baron selected the two best representatives to send off to his homeland. Today there are twenty-seven recognized species within the African violet genus.

Saintpaulia Species and Their Descriptions

The Educational Committee for the 31st annual African Violet Society of American Convention/Show prepared this collection of the *Saintpaulia* (abbreviated as *S.*) species and their descriptions. The committee consisted of Mary Mathew Mahen, Virginia Fisler Meyer, Lois Newton Russell, and Edd Stretch Smith. Reprinted from the January 1978 issue of the *African Violet Magazine.*

1. S. brevipilosa

Growing as a small single-crowned plant with tightly bunched leaves, this one usually hides its flowers with its rounded leaves which are thin and light-green. Abundantly borne, the soft-purple flowers, dark-centered, are not long-lived. Moderate light, temperature and moisture are to its liking.

2. S. confusa

Quite ample moisture and very good drainage are a must! An 1895 discovery, taken from the gneiss rock formation near Mount Mlinga some 15 miles from Mount Tongwe, this plant is one of the two original species grown in Germany. Deep-purple flowers are produced infrequently in abundance. It may be grown small, but is much more impressive as a large multiple-crowned plant. Appreciable results are evident with 1,000 to 1,200 foot candle-light exposure.

3. S. difficilis

Chartreuse leaves on long, bent petioles make this 1939 discovery a distinctive one. Medium-blue flowers appear profusely on an upright single crown: its habitat was more widespread than many of the species since it was known in an area between Kenya and Tanzania in three different and distinct areas.

4. *S. diplotricha* Number 6

5. *S. diplotricha* Number 7

6. *S. diplotricha* Number 0

The differences between these three are so technical and trivial that they are best left to the taxonomists, i.e., the length or angle of a hair, and so on.

Coming from various altitudes in the Usambara Mountains, it is a small rosette plant; single-crowned, dark-leaved, thick-fleshed, and bears appealing water-colored lilac flowers. Don't overwater.

7. *S. goetzeana*

From all known records this tiny and temperamental species, found nestled among mosses in the primeval forst of the Lukwangule Plateau, has blossomed only once since its discovery seventy-seven years ago.

Success in growing this plant is to be commended. Forming tiny clumps of countless rosettes, it will probably produce two or three diminutive flowers of palest lilac hue—should that day ever come. It is a very weak-rooted plant, and requires temperatures ranging from as low as 40 degrees F. to 90 degrees F. with fluctuating 40 percent to 70 percent humidity.

8. *S. grandifolia* Number 299

9. *S. grandifolia* Number 237

Both plants usually grow single-crowned. They become quite large, as their name implies, and are most handsome with their very large, crinkled, waferthin, elliptical leaves growing somewhat upright on lengthy pliable petioles. Quite floriferous for a species; the blossoms are crisp, blue-violet in color. Discovered in the Usambara Mountains.

10. *S. grotei*

This most fascinating gesneriad should, perhaps, be considered a true vine because it can attain a height or length of over three feet. Coming from the Amani vicinity near Tanzania, it grew in dense shade with abundant moisture and excellent drainage. Found in 1920, it has not been appreciated for its hybridizing potential until quite lately. Bearing its two-toned, blue-violet flowers rather few in number on flimsy peduncles, it becomes more prolific with exposure to higher than normal temperatures (78 to 85 degrees F.). Long, rampant petioles are distinctively bark-brown in color and terminate in flat, rounded, dentate leaves, varied in size from a slight one inch to over three inches. Tiny swellings on the plant's stem are nodes which may produce air roots during periods of high humidity. Cuttings root quite well, rapidly and easily. *S. grotei* may be trained in growth pattern, either upward in a trellised effect or downward as a weeper.

11. *S. inconspicua*

This elusive member grew sparsely in an Uluguru Mountain forest. Not known until 1932, it was a frail trailer and bore small blue-spotted white flowers atypical of other species. It is now believed extinct since the bombings of Germany during World War II. First classed as a *Didymocarpus,* it is felt that this plant could lend much to the future of African violet breeding programs—should another ever come forth.

12. *S. intermedia*

Blue flowers, five to seven in number, are borne in modest numbers on this interesting deviate. As its name implies, it grows somewhere between a trailing plant and a rosette one. Small, round, olive-green serrate leaves are inclined to spoon or cup in a lotus-leaf pattern.

13. *S. ionantha*

The first species to be named, it was later found that some of the plants were really what became *S. confusa*. These two have lent more to today's cultivars than any others.

A large grower, *S. ionantha* has dark-green, glossy, quilted, serrate leaves and clusters of blue-violet flowers, numerous in count. It endures summer heat well, having evolved in torrid surroundings. Although leaves cup upward, they have a tendency to droop slightly as temperatures approach 80 degrees F.

14. *S. magungensis*
15. *S. magungensis,* var. *minima*
16. *S. magungensis,* var. *occidentalis*

The foothills of the Usambara Mountains at Magunga are now under cultivation; the only area where this species and its variants grew. Now extinct in Africa, this procumbent branched plant continues to root as it touches soil and readily produces new clumps. Two to four medium violet-blue flowers top all peduncles, which are numerous. It is a most valuable addition to the plant breeder's collection!

17. *S. nitida*

Dark-leaved, Tanzania-borne, *S. nitida* is a natural spreader. It remains small, and its flowers too are dark. Ample moisture and only modest light are to its liking and it prefers coolness.

18. *S. orbicularis*
19. *S. orbicularis* var. *purpurea*

Found in 1916 at 4,000 to 7,000-foot heights in the western Usambara Mountains, this one likes cold nights and very hot days (45 to 90 degrees F. range). Growing handsomely upright as a multiple plant (or single-crowned) its dark-green, shiny leaves are small and nearly round. Light lilac, dark-centered flowers are in abundance much of the time.

20. *S. pendula*
21. *S. pendula* var. *kizarae*

Many-crowned and trailing, this lavender-flowered, round-leaved, light-green member is a thirsty and hungry beauty. It will share the spotlight with others so long as it receives an ample portion for itself. Like all temperamental stars, it refuses to perform if its demands are not met. "Sister" kizarae plays the supporting role.

22. *S. pusilla*

The smallest species ever found, *S pusilla* is now regretfully believed lost

30

forever since the World War II Berlin bombings. The minute mauve-and-white flowers were true jewels, staged above tiny purple-backed triangular leaves. Less difficult and temperamental than *S goetzeana*, the plant stands alone in diminutive greatness.

23. *S. rupicola*

With slanting and "suckering" tendencies, this species is most suitable for "totem-pole" or "strawberry jar" culture. It is not difficult in cultivation and is medium-blue flowered.

24. *S. shumensis*

Single-crowned and suckering freely, this small bright-green plant blooms palest-blue flowers in sparse numbers. Reduce nitrogen and increase light to inhibit suckering.

25. *S. teitensis*

The species grows upright and single-crowned, with dark-green, shiny, pointed red-backed leaves and lone, light-blue violet flowers. Its outer leaves tend to spoon and are brittle and thick. Medium light and moisture are to its liking.

26. *S. tongwensis*

Reaching maturity early, this species grows symmetrical, upright, rarely has suckers, and easily remains single-crowned. Freely producing copious quantities of soft-blue flower, this one appears to be the strongest and most robust of all the species. It is not a demanding plant, and its pleasant nature will lend encouragement while you try some other more difficult ones.

27. *S. velutina*

As its name implies, this one is a velvety reddish-green plant. Especially appealing for its ease of growth and flowering, the flat rosette produces large quantities of medium-violet, red-centered blossoms in all but the hottest months. Grow it near the edge of a bench, if lighted, or in a northeast exposure. Don't overfeed or overwater.

28. *S. amaniensis*

A noted African violet taxonomist, Mr. B. L. Burtt, has reclassified S. *amaniensis*—frequently mentioned as a separate variety—as only a variation of *S. magugensis.* Two other possible species not yet classified as such are: *S. House of Amani.*

A most beautiful single-crowned plant, which has so much going for it. Never having been properly identified or classified as a true species, it throws numerous trusses of medium lavender-blue, short-lived flowers numbering five to seven per stalk. Flower drop can be noticeably reduced by feeding with an unusually high phosphate diet. Pointed, quilted, dark-green, dentate to scallop leaves are enhanced by red backs and petioles. To lengthen peduncles, grow the plant about two feet from an overhead light source with fourteen to sixteen hours exposure daily.

29. *S. Sigi Falls*

Along with *S. House of Amani,* not yet declared a true species, this hardy pubescent beauty blooms freely. Thick ovate leaves vary in size; they are handsomely veined and red-backed. Grows easily. Try it for fun.

Individual varieties of African violets for sale are too numerous to list here. It would take several pages to tell you about each one. Chapter 13 contains a listing of many of the more popular African violets now available. If you are interested in obtaining a list of all the varieties, write to the African Violet Society of America, P. O. Box 1326, Knoxville, Tennessee 37901. Ask for their Master Variety List of all the registered African violets.

An up-to-date listing of the current, most popular plants among the African violet hobbyists is available from two sources. Each spring the African Violet Society prints the "Best 100," an elite group of favorite African violets from the last year. Write to the above address to obtain this list. The second choice for up-to-date listings of favorite plants is the bi-monthly magazine *Gesneriad Saintpaulia News,* which lists the "Favorite Fifty" African violets in each issue. You may reach this publication office by writing to P. O. Box 549, Knoxville, Tennessee 37901.

African violet hobbyists are constantly working with their plants, crossbreeding them and developing newer and more interesting African violets. Whenever a new feature is discovered, another variety is born. These man-made varieties are referred to as "cultivars." Anytime this word shows up in the description of an African violet, you know that some enthusiastic grower has had a hand in the development of the plant.

Parade of African Violets

Naming a new African violet is at the discretion of the person who has developed the plant. Anything goes, so long as no one else has used the same name. You'll find it very entertaining just to look over a list of the registered African violets and note the names which have been selected. Sometimes the name will give you a hint as to some special feature displayed by a particular African violet, such as 'Blue Royal,' 'Gypsy Pink' and 'Lavendar Delight.' Obviously these three names refer to the color of the blossoms. Now on the other hand, names like 'Happy Harold,' 'Jeanmarie,' 'Hanky Panky,' and 'Earth Angel' don't tell you anything about the characteristics of the African violets which carry these names. Most of the names fall into this latter category.

I have compiled two shorts lists of names used by African violet hobbyists and commercial growers so you can get a good idea of the free and easy way names are bestowed on new varieties. After glancing over the lists you can readily see that if you ever develop a new African violet you can name it after your wife, dog, cat, favorite drink, an old expression, or even tag it with a descriptive term hinting about its special feature of which you are so proud.

FLOWER COLOR

White	Purple	Red	Pink
Blizzard Supreme	After Dark	Bullseye	Baby Pink
Crystal	Checkmate	Dixie Magic	Blush Love
Frosted Snow Prince	French Knight	Fire Hazard	Coral Glow
Ivory Buttons	Indigo Maid	Heartaches	Lady Luck
Pearl Moon	Night Rider	Prince Royal	Las Vegas
Snow	Royal Token	Red Frost	Pink Pirate
Pure Innocence	The General	Sunrise Chalet	Playmate
White Cup	Royal Fluff	U-All-Come	Supremacy
White Tango	Sultry Purple	Winter Wine	Terrific

PLANT SIZE

Miniature (6" or less)	Semiminiature (6" to 8")	Standard (8" to 16")	Large (over 16")
Midget Mischief	Andy Griffiths	Affectionate	After Five
Knee High	Button Trinket	Babette	Barbara's Christie
Tiny Gypsy	Candy Trinket	Debbie Sue	Bright Sails
Tiny Ellie	Dancing Doll	Flamingo	First Kiss
Little Precious	Little Miss Texas	Red Star	Jimeney Crickets
Sweetie Pie	White Moon	Albert the Second	Purple Pride

Creating New Varieties

For years professional plant breeders and hobbyists have worked with African violets, developing new and exciting characteristics and improving on nature's original work. Through their efforts a wide array of African violets are available from which the avid grower can choose. Plants with double blossoms, ruffled petals, deeply serrated leaves, blossoms with streaks through the petals, miniature plants, leaves covered with hairy-like projections, large blossoms—all these improvements and many more are the work of growers dedicated to improving the almost perfect features of the plant.

Without a doubt the plant breeders will continue working with the African violets, trying to bring out some new feature that has not yet surfaced in any plant. The genetics of the plant are very complicated (as they are in all living plants and animals) and a hidden gene might just emerge without any warning and produce a new variety.

If you want to be a creative African violet grower you should join the ranks of the active plant breeders. Start your own crossbreeding program with African violets and discover one of the real joys of gardening. The pleasure of developing new plants, of which there are none quite like yours, is well worth the time and effort you will spend in the process. You should be aware of the fact that it may take years before you reach your goal of creating a new African violet with that special feature you want to be the focal point of the plant. Sometimes a sport will show up in your collection of plants and the time period will be considerably shortened.

To be a successful plant breeder requires you to be very selective. You will almost always be working from seed, and therefore a large number of plants are involved. Each fertilized seed pod is capable of producing 400 to 600 seeds. So from a single cross to one flower you could end up with hundreds of plants. Fertilize two flowers, and you double the number of seed and potential plants.

You will have to select the feature you are interested in developing in your African violets. Then you must get rid of all those plants which do not display that feature. For example, if you are trying to obtain a pure-red flower, you would toss out or give away all those plants that did not produce flowers with some shade of red in them. It's going to be tough, but you must do it or your home will become overrun with African violets.

Keeping records is extremely important when doing any crossbreeding. After you have finished developing a new plant, you want to be able to trace your steps back to the parent plants. Don't let this phase of the job scare you because it is an easy task. To do the job of keeping track of your plants, tag each one and list where the pollen was obtained to fertilize the blossoms. An example of what a tag may have written on it would be:

with the X meaning ''crossed with.'' This tag will be removed when the seed matures and stays with the seed through planting, germination, and the growth of the new plants. When plants are put into individual pots, each will be tagged so it can be traced back to the parent plants. Then if you cross-pollinate any of these plants with other plants, the combination of plants used will be recorded on a tag and assigned to the new seed when it is mature and ready for harvesting.

Your ultimate goal, then, is to produce a new hybrid African violet through a well-planned crossbreeding program. Hybrid is the term used for any new plant developed from crossing two different African violets which results in offspring with features differing uniquely from those of its parent plants. Should you become serious in your endeavors to create a new African violet, you should go to the library and read some books on genetics. You will find the subject not only fascinating but also gain an insight into how African violets have evolved through eons of time to their present place of distinction as the most popular indoor flowering plant.

Pollination of Flowers

All African violets can be crossed with each other since they are closely related. Both the domestic and wild African violets can be used in your breeding work to develop new traits in your plants. At first, stick with the new improved varieties and your chances of success will be greatly increased.

For your breeding work select those features in a plant that you personally feel should be spotlighted, then use plants which prominently display these features. Collect pollen from a plant that has the desirable qualities and pollinate the blossoms of another African violet which has similar traits. By doing this you are attempting to intensify these features in the next generation. Some special features you may choose to work with are: color, size, and shape of the flower, foliage color, number of flowers produced on a plant, how long the flowers last, and overall appearance of the African violet.

Pollination of the blossoms can be accomplished anytime of the year so long as the pollen is mature. Look at the anthers of the blossom. If they are very yellow and the powder-like pollen inside sticks to your finger, then it is mature. The female portion of the plant (pistil) will be mature enough for fertilization from the pollen if the yellow anthers have ripe pollen in them. A sure sign that the pistil is mature is if a sticky substance oozes from the tip (stigma) of the pistil. It is usually safe to assume, if you want to take a small gamble, that when the developing flower has reached the same size as the older ones on the plant it is mature enough for use in a breeding program.

Although pollination is possible anytime, certain times of the year are better than others. African violet growth seems to be best in the spring and fall when the temperatures do not become extremely hot in your house. This allows the seed to develop at a normal pace and insures a better quality of seed produced by the plant. Keep in mind that a plant developing seed in its pods should not be overwatered. As a plant produces seeds, the moisture content of the soil should be kept drier than normal.

When doing breeding work, it does not matter how many flowers on a single plant are pollinated. The development of seedpods does not harm an African violet. I would not pollinate the flowers of one plant with pollen from more than one other plant because it is difficult to keep track of which individual flower was pollinated by what donor plant.

Any flowers not pollinated should be removed to prevent accidental pollination. If pollen from unknown sources enters the picture, your breeding program is in for trouble. You'll have seeds and plants which you cannot trace to any particular plants and ruin your chances for accurate records.

Actual pollination of plants occurs when pollen lands or is placed on the tip of the pistil. Remember, we are talking about a sticky substance present on the stigma. It serves a very important function. This viscous ooze makes it very easy for the pollen to adhere to the female portion of the blossom.

Once the pollen has become imbedded on the stigma it sends a germ tube down through the style of the pistil into the ovary. Here the male and female gametes fuse and the seed of the new plant begins to develop. First visual signs of a successful cross will begin developing in one to two weeks when the ovary begins to enlarge. All this sounds very simple, but it really is a complicated process that occurs everyday in nature. Numerous plant scientists and geneticists have devoted their entire lives to the study of this one plant phenomenon..

Development of the Seed

After the fertilization process occurs in the ovary of the African violet, you can sit back and let nature do the rest of the work for you. All it takes now is time for the seeds to form, and for you to have the patience to wait for them. The length of time varies according to the variety with which you are working, and the time of year when the flowers were pollinated. Miniatures require about three months; the semiminiatures, standards, and Supremes take five to six months for the seed-riping process to be completed.

As the seeds are maturing, the seedpod swells, elongates, and remains a light-green color in the early stages of the seed development. Don't worry if the seedpod appears to have stopped growing and no other visible signs of growth are noticeable. Plenty is happening inside where the seeds are busily growing.

During this time the flower stalk will begin curling and twisting itself up. You can visually tell when the seeds are ripe by watching the swollen seedpod. A mature seedpod will be shriveled up, dried, and brownish in color. At this stage the pods are ready for removal from the plant. Once the seedpods have been removed, you should pace them in a dry warm spot where there is good air circulation. This will allow the seeds to dry out and complete the maturation process in two to four weeks. An envelope makes a handy storage container for holding the pods. Should the pods break open the seed will still be trapped, avoiding a loss when you have been waiting months to obtain seed from your plants. Seeds can completely mature on the plant; but if the pods erupt, you will lose most of the seed.

Seed of the African violets is so fine that the best way to describe it is to compare it with dust particles. As previously mentioned, there are 750,000 seeds per ounce. It would take 1,500 individual African violet blossoms to produce one ounce of seed, assuming that each one produces 500 seeds.

When you are ready to remove seeds from the pods, spread a large piece of white paper on a table. The dark seeds can easily be seen against this white backdrop. Break the pods over the paper; this will allow you to be certain of collecting all the seeds from each pod.

Normally seeds will germinate and new seedlings emerge in twenty-one to twenty-eight days when the temperature is 65 to 75 degrees F. In the *African Violet Magazine,* one grower reported the following sequence of time for seeds to develop into flowering plants: The seeds were planted and maintained under ideal conditions, allowing them to germinate in twenty-five days. In six months' time the African violets had six healthy leaves; by the end of another month, buds and flowers had developed.

The number of seeds that may germinate from your plants is hard to predict. If you have everything perfect—temperature, moisture, humidity, air circulation, light—anywhere from 50 to 100 percent of the seeds will germinate. Remember, though, that some seeds just won't germinate and others are destined to become beautiful African violet plants. Don't give up if your first attempt at collecting seeds is not as successful as you had hoped. Perseverance is the real key to success in any breeding program where you are trying to develop your own seed with which to work.

Genes and Chromosomes

What controls the color of the flower, its size and shape? Why does a plant's offspring have the same ruffled leaf margins as its parents? Questions of this type often arise when someone begins wondering how African violets progress from generation to generation displaying the same characteristics.

The answers to such questions are found in microscopic structures called chromosomes which are found in every living cell of a plant. These rodlike structures are composed of many smaller building blocks called genes. Genes are simply a specific chemical arrangement or composition that tells the plant which features to display. A chromosome, then, is composed of a series of these chemical patterns (genes) hooked together end to end, forming the rodlike shape which can be seen under a powerful microscope. The arrangement of the genes on the chromosomes determines what characteristics will be featured in each new African violet plant.

Let's back up for a moment and see how the chromosomes are transferred from one plant to another. The pollen grains, found in the stamens, each have one-half of the total set of chromosomes needed for plant development. The other half of the set is stored in the ovaries (located at the base of the pistil) of the flower. When the pollen lands on the pistil and the germ tube starts growing down to the ovary, the partial set of chromosomes in the pollen grain migrate down the germ tube into the ovary. The two half sets of chromosomes are then united in the egg cells found in the ovary, and fertilization has occurred.

Plant variation in African violets is due to the many different possible combinations of the genes located along the length of the rodlike chromosomes. It is this ever-possible variation in plants that keeps plant breeders and hobbyists busy and hopeful. Out of thousands of crosses, breeders may consider themselves lucky if eventually a single new African violet hybrid is discovered.

Most African violets have the same number of chromosomes (thirty) present in every cell. There are a few varieties—Supremes, DuPont, and Amazons—which have twice as many chromosomes (sixty). The larger than normal flowers and extra thick leaves exhibited by these plants are a good indication of the extra set of chromosomes.

How does a mutant or sport occur? Mutations in African violets will occur in the next generation. This will cause the plant's appearance to be dif-If a single gene and its chemical composition is changed, a mutation will occur in the next generation. This will cause the plant's appearance to be different from the parents. Several African violet varieties being grown today were obtained this way. Some mutant features seen are: red-and-white flowers, double-petaled blossoms, fringed flowers, and girl-type foliage.

Dominant and Recessive Genes

When fertilization takes place in the ovary of a flower the chromosomes are paired, matching up like sets of genes so the various characteristics of the new plant can be determined. These genes are either dominant or recessive. When a particular characteristic controlled by the genes is always overpowering it is said to be the dominant trait. The subdued genes are called recessive.

Remember, when talking about genes and their control over plant features we are considering a pair of genes—united in the ovary after the fertilization of the flower has occurred. It is important to keep this in mind because of the way dominance works in controlling which characteristics will come to the surface in new plants. For the recessive gene characteristics to show up in a plant it is necessary for both genes in the matched pair to be recessive. The dominant characteristic is displayed in the plant if only one gene in the pair is dominant.

A good example of dominant and recessive traits can be seen if we look at a cross between two African violets with blue flowers. Both plants also carry the recessive gene for red flowers. In the following examples, the capital letter indicates the dominant gene, and a small letter is used to denote the recessive gene.

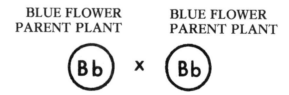

BLUE FLOWER   BLUE FLOWER
PARENT PLANT   PARENT PLANT

Bb   x   Bb

By crossing two plants which have the above pairs of genes located on the chromosome there are four possible random combinations of genes that controls flower color in the next generation. Which genes are carried from one plant to the next is a matter of simple luck. Below are the possibilities and the color of the flower which each possible combination of genes will produce.

BLUE FLOWER	BLUE FLOWER	BLUE FLOWER	RED FLOWER
BB	Bb	Bb	bb

From this example you can see that the blue flowering color is the dominant characteristic. So long as a single dominant gene is involved, the blue flower will show up in the next generation. Two recessive genes produce a red-flowered African violet. In a cross of this nature, you could expect three-fourths of the new plants to have blue flowers and one-fourth to have red flowers.

Recessive characteristics can remain hidden for generation after generation before surfacing. For this reason don't be surprised if you cross-pollinate plants for several years before some unexpected trait pops up. To illustrate this point suppose you select two plants, both with blue flowers, and begin a breeding program. One plant carries a recessive gene b for red flowers, and the other plant has two dominant blue genes B. Don't forget that the genes we are talking about are being carried in the pollen and in the ovary of the plants. So until the right pollen grain carrying the recessive red gene trait b fertilizes a plant with the recessive gene b, red flowers will not be produced.

The genes present in the pollen and ovary of the plant determine the possible characteristics that will develop. In the first generation of the illustration had the pollen from the plant with Bb genes fertilized the ovary of the plant where the genes Bb were programed, the presence of the nonblue flower could have occurred in the second generation.

Genetics, the study of heredity and how it occurs, is a fascinating subject. Once you have an understanding of this science the doors of the past and future are open to you. With some experience, you will learn to accurately predict the characteristics that will show up in your new African violets.

BLUE FLOWERED   BLUE FLOWERED
PARENT PLANT   PARENT PLANT

(Bb)   x   (BB)

1ST
GENERATION   BB   BB   Bb   Bb   ALL BLUE FLOWERS

(BB)   x   (Bb)

2D
GENERATION   BB   BB   Bb   Bb   ALL BLUE FLOWERS

(BB)   x   (Bb)

3D
GENERATION   BB   Bb   Bb   BB   ALL BLUE FLOWERS

(Bb)   x   (Bb)

4TH
GENERATION   BB   Bb   Bb   bb

BLUE FLOWERS   RED FLOWERS

40

Hybridizing Variegated Plants

African violets with variegated leaves are becoming increasingly popular. The contrasting green-and-white leaves give the plant an elegant appearance. Even when these plants don't live up to their reputation and fail to produce an abundance of blossoms, the green-and-white foliage insures an attractive and unusual houseplant. In fact many homeowners grow these variegated African violets as much for their foliage as for the lovely blossoms they are capable of producing.

If you are going to work with variegated African violets in a breeding program you must know what causes variegated leaves, and which techniques are necessary to produce a new plant with the variegated-leaf characteristic.

To produce new plants with variegated foliage there is one rule you *must* follow to be successful. RULE: A variegated plant must be used in the breeding program, and it has to be the plant that produces the seed. For example, if you have two plants, one with and one without variegated foliage, you must transfer the pollen from the anthers of the nonvariegated plant to the stigma of the variegated plant. Transferring pollen from the variegated plant to the nonvariegated plant *will not* produce offspring with variegated foliage.

Let's take a brief look at the African violet's internal makeup to discover why the variegated plant has to be the one to produce the seed. The secret to this unusual feature is locked away in the germ cells of the plant. A close examination of a pollen grain and an egg (mother) cell will unlock the door to one of nature's most interesting mysteries.

The pollen produced in the anthers is a mass of proteinaceous material encased in a thin-walled shell. Floating around inside this shell are the chromosomes which carry one-half of the genetic code for the creation of the next generation. Pollen grains do not contain any genetic information or extraneous materials that will have any influence on whether the plants will or will not have variegated foliage. You must examine the plant that produces the seed to discover how variegation occurs in African violets.

The egg cell of the seed plant is a more complex structure than the pollen grain. Besides containing the nucleus with its genetic information, there are also other structures floating around within the egg cell. These structures, called chloroplasts, are the bodies within a plant's cells that cause it to be green.

When the chromosomes from the pollen grain and egg cell come together in the seed plant, the chloroplasts become part of the new seed cells formed from the union of the chromosomes. The green color in the leaves of the new plant is then governed by the amount of chloroplasts found floating around the egg cell in the seed plant. A variegated plant has an egg cell with very few chloroplasts, and a nonvariegated African violet has a very large number of chloroplasts in its egg cell. This is the reason why the variegated plant must be the seed plant. The smaller the amount of chloroplasts assimilated in the forming seed, the greater the variegation will be in the

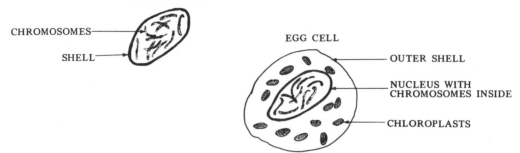

POLLEN GRAIN

CHROMOSOMES

SHELL

EGG CELL

OUTER SHELL

NUCLEUS WITH
CHROMOSOMES INSIDE

CHLOROPLASTS

The differences between the two reproductive cells of an African violet are shown here. The number of chloroplasts present in the egg cell determines whether the plant's leaves will be variegated or nonvariegated.

foliage of the plant. Large quantities of chloroplasts would cause plants to have solid-green leaves.

Retaining the variegated foliage in your new plants should not be a difficult task now that you understand how this feature is controlled by the African violet plant. Just remember the rule: A variegated plant must be used in the breeding program, and it has to be the plant which produces the seed—and you'll always be successful.

Registering New Plants

One question that always comes to mind is: when crossbreeding or pollinating African violets, when will I know whether I have a new plant that should be named and registered? The African violet you are thinking of registering must pass a "trueness test"; it simply must always produce the same identical plant time after time when it is being propagated vegetatively (leaf cuttings). At least three generations of plants must pass the trueness test before you consider a plant for registration.

Now you know the test all new African violets must undergo before they can be registered, what new features do you look for before starting the procedure? Coloring and size of the flowers are major features in which you should be particularly interested. Look for unusual colored petals and larger than normal flowers. New plants with uniform color and a rosette growth habit which is symmetrical are highly desirable.

Registration of all African violets is handled by the African Violet Society of America. In 1966 the International Commission for the Registration of Horticultural Plants recognized this dedicated organization as being capable of such a monumental task. Information and a guide telling you how to go about the registration procedure can be obtained from the Society.

42

3
Watering Your African Violets

Watering African violets can be a very simple chore, or it can become very frustrating. This is especially true for the new African violet owner who has never before tried to grow these lovely plants. Probably no other phase of African violet care causes more headaches than setting up a routine watering schedule to insure healthy plants. Correct watering is an art that evades many growers who are haphazard in the care they give their plants. Overwatering and underwatering are two common ailments which afflict many African violet plants.

If your plants suddenly become shabby looking or sickly the first question fellow growers will ask is, "How have you been watering them?" After you answer the question, about half of the "plant doctors" will tell you to water the plants more frequently; the other half will insist that you have been overwatering the plants.

So who is correct? Each plant has its own needs based on temperature, light intensity (brightness), fertilizing program, pot size, and the humidity around the plants. You must learn to adapt the watering schedule to meet the needs of your plants. At the same time you may be certain that your African violets are learning to adapt to your system of watering. It is just a case of becoming acquainted with each other's habits. Once this happens you will have healthy, happy plants worthy of display anywhere in your home.

Water Essential to Growth of Plants

Before looking into all the different aspects of watering African violets, let's take a few minutes here to learn what the water does for a plant. Many plants are composed of 80 to 90 percent moisture, and only 10 to 20 percent solid matter. This can be easily determined by weighing freshly cut plants, then placing them in an oven to dry them out. The difference in the weight is the measurement of water content contained in the plant's tissues.

Once the water has been taken from the soil and moves into the plant leaves, its most significant contribution is in the manufacture of food (photosynthesis) for the plant. A water molecule consists of two hydrogen and one oxygen molecule. In a complex photochemical reaction the light from the sun splits the water molecule into two different types of molecules. These hydrogen and oxygen atoms are then used in the manufacturing of plant food (sugars, starches, cellulose).

The process of this complex splitting of water molecules is called Hill's Reaction. The next time one of your botanist friends tries to overwhelm you with his knowledge on how photosynthesis works in a plant, wait until the appropriate time and then say, "Oh, you must be referring to Hill's Reaction, where the sunlight strikes the water and splits it up so the plant can manufacture its own food." While your friend is recovering from the shock of your making such an astute comment, tactfully change the subject.

The plant nutrients in the soil must be able to get to the plant so the roots can absorb them. It is true that roots will grow to their food, but most nutrients move through the soil to the roots by water. After the nutrients are in the plant it is again the water which carries the nutrients throughout the plant.

Test Soil Before Watering

How do you determine when it is time to water your African violets? Experience will be your best guide. Trying to describe an exact watering schedule for your plants is an impossible task. As previously mentioned, this will depend on many different conditions which exist for each plant. I shall give you a few guidelines you may follow, but beyond that you must learn the needs of your own plants.

The touch test with your fingers is the best technique to use for determining if you need to water. Be careful not to damage the plant while reaching under the leaves to feel the soil. If the soil is too dry it will feel crusty. A gentle thrust of the finger into the soil will show if it is also too hard for good plant growth when the soil is dry. Seldom will you have to worry about hard soil since your African violets are probably being grown in a highly organic soil mixture.

When you remove your finger some traces of soil will have stuck. If soil particles are damp-looking (dark in color) the plant will do well for another day without water. If soil particles are glistening with moisture then the plant has received too much water. Let the soil dry out for a day or two and test it again before watering.

Humidity, temperature, light intensity, type soil mixture, size of pot, location of plant in your home, time of the year—all these factors will affect your watering schedule. All are variables which mean that you must check your plants daily to determine when they need water.

44

Always use the "touch test" to determine when to water African violets. A few dark-colored soil particles will cling to your finger if the soil is still sufficiently moist.

Setting Up a Watering Schedule

Each African violet grower has a preference to the best time of day for watering. Mornings or evenings seem to be the two most popular times. In the morning the plant is getting ready for another day's active growth and a drink of water gets it off to a good start. The humidity around the plant is usually highest in the morning and this, coupled with a good watering, produces ideal growing conditions for African violets.

Evening watering advocates feel that by watering late in the day they avoid spotting the leaves when water is accidentally spilled on them. It takes bright sunshine to cause spotting (burns) of the leaves, and if the sun has already gone down for the night this problem is solved. Of course using a watering container with a long narrow spout and being careful solves the problem in the first place and there would be no need to worry about the sunshine.

How Much Water

Each plant variety has its own water requirements; and even in a given

45

variety of African violets, individual species must be handled differently. In this respect African violets are similar to humans, each having a personality all its own. You must get to know a plant's personality if it is to thrive well in your home.

Overwatering has led to the demise of more African violets than any other single cause. It is the most common plant problem known to indoor gardeners. Too much water causes waterlogged soils and severely retards the root system development. If this condition is allowed to continue for an extended period of time, the plants will turn yellow and slowly die.

Let's briefly consider how waterlogged soil kills a plant. If a plant is to be happy growing in a particular soil mixture it must have a good oxygen supply present in that soil. This oxygen is taken up by the roots and used in the conversion of the plant's stored food into energy it needs for growing. Overwatering forces all the oxygen out of the soil and causes a plant to fail to produce the necessary energy to sustain its healthy growth. If this condition is allowed to remain for too long a period, the plant slowly starves to death.

The amount of water you use for each watering will vary according to the African violet needs. Plants growing in two and a half to three inch diameter pots should receive an average of a quarter cup of water per day. Be sure to test the soil to determine if any water is needed. Larger pots will require a little more water, and you should allow for this. Let any excess water drain out the bottom of the pot through the drain hole. Discard this water.

You are overwatering if a lot of water comes out the bottom drain hole. This washes the nutrients from the soil and eventually will cause problems for the plant if you don't plan for it. Just a very small amount (five to ten drops) of water should seep out. When this quantity of water does drip out then the plant is properly watered.

Double Watering

Many African violet growers follow the practice of watering their plants twice at about a thirty-minute interval. More water is applied at each watering than the soil can hold. The excess is allowed to drip away. This is done for two reasons. The water moving through the soil will leach out any excess fertilizer salts which have accumulated in the soil, and help to prevent any chances of salt damages to the plant roots. The second watering insures that all the soil in the pot is thoroughly wetted, causing the soil to swell and push against the sides of the pot. This prevents water from running down the sides of the pot and directly out the drain hole without wetting the soil.

If you use this double watering technique you will have to take care in keeping your African violets supplied with sufficient plant food so their growth won't be retarded. Also, let the soil dry out sufficiently to allow plenty of oxygen to move into the roots before the next watering.

Quality of Water

African violets have a tropical origin where the temperatures are always warm, and rainfall is the main source of moisture. These facts should be kept in mind when you are about to give your plant its next drink. The quality of the water is often overlooked, and since the kitchen tap is so convenient it automatically becomes the source of water for most indoor gardeners. It used to be safe to assume that if the water was good enough to drink then it was good enough for plants. Now, with all the modern conveniences, this may or may not be the case.

Usually the city water supply or, if you live in the country, your well water, is referred to as being hard. This means it contains a high amount of dissolved salts such as calcium, iron and magnesium. To solve this problem, soft-water conditioners are installed in most homes today. A soft-water conditioner removes the hard salts from water as it moves through the tank. In this process, sodium is released into the water. The amount is so small you can't taste it in your drinking water, but the sodium will cause a salt problem for your African violets if soft water is used for a prolonged period of time. Eventually the sodium will accumulate in the soil to a toxic level.

There are several ways to get around this problem if you have soft water in your home. Usually the water which is plumbed to the outside water taps for yard work has not passed through a soft-water conditioner, so you could draw your water from this source. However, it will still contain the hard salts, iron, calcium, and magnesium which can eventually accumulate in the soil; but this should not present you with any problems if you let a little water drip out the drain hole at each watering.

Rainwater is another source for you to use when watering African violets. It is free of harmful chemicals, provided you do not live next to a factory or in an industrial area. Rainwater does have some nutrients present in it. As it lazily falls from the clouds, it absorbs nitrogen and sulfur from the air. These two nutrients are important to the health of all plants. Since very few of you have cisterns or rain barrels anymore, chances are that you won't want to be bothered with collecting rainwater. If you live in a humid and wet part of the country or have ever visited one of these areas, you are well aware of the moisture present in the air. The relative humidity is often higher than the temperature. This moist air offers an excellent source of pure water for use on your African violets.

Air conditioners and dehumidifiers are used extensively in humid regions to make life more comfortable for the inhabitants. The moisture removed from the air is almost 100 percent pure water, free from any harmful salts or toxic chemicals. I have used condensated water for my indoor plants and African violets and have never had any problems caused by the quality of water from this source. I do remember occasionally to add plant food to the water to insure that my plants always have an adequate supply of food available.

Water temperature is an important criteria you must remember if you want your African violets to look gorgeous all the time. Remember, these are tropical plants which are used to warm rainwater. The first rule to religiously follow is always use room temperature water. Just think how you felt the last time you went swimming and jumped into a pool. The shock of the cold water sent chills throughout your body. Your first thought was to yell back to your friends and warn them. Cold water has the same effect on African violets but they aren't able to shout a warning. Instead they may just refuse to flower anymore or develop brown spots on their leaves. Cold water will also retard growth. When cold water touches the roots it actually shocks them. In turn this affects the overall performance of the plant and ruins its appearance.

When I said that water should be at room temperature I was referring to the rooms in which you are comfortable and not a cold basement or garage. Water temperature of between 68 and 72 degrees is ideal for your African violets. If water is 5 to 7 degrees cooler or warmer it won't hurt the plant; if the water is 10 degrees higher or lower than room temperature, don't use it. Keep the water in a container long enough to reach room temperature.

The best procedure to follow is to keep the water in a container for twenty-four hours before you plan to use it. This not only allows it to reach room temperature but acquires an additional side benefit. Most cities add chlorine to their water supply to purify it for drinking. This water, when used for watering plants, may cause them some problems. The chlorine itself does not harm African violets, but it kills the soil organisms responsible for breaking up plant nutrients into the individual elements which the plant uses as food.

By allowing the water to stand in an open container for twenty-four hours before using it, the chlorine evaporates from the water as a harmless gas. If it is necessary occasionally to water with chlorinated water it will not harm your African violets. Only continuous use of chlorinated water will eventually cause your African violets any problems.

Different Methods of Watering

A sure way to arouse a good debate among African violet hobbyists is to bring up the topic of which way the plant should be watered—from the top or from the bottom. Both sides will declare that their way is the only way, but the African violets would tell you it doesn't really matter which way you water them. What does concern African violets is how carefully the water is applied.

Top watering must be done with caution—being careful not to get any water on the plant's leaves or on its crown. Buy a watering container with a long, narrow spout. This will allow you to direct the water to the soil, not on the plant. Be careful not to wash all the soil away from the crown of the plant.

If you should accidentally spill any water drops on the leaves, remove the plant from direct sunlight until the water evaporates. Drops of water act as a small magnifying lens and will allow the sun's rays to burn the leaves. This will cause small brown spots on the foliage.

Applying water from the top should always be the method to use when dealing with young plants with small root systems. This way you can direct

Top watering plants helps to prevent the build-up of toxic salts at the soil surface. Be careful not to spill any water onto the leaves.

the water to the soil directly over the plant roots, wetting only that soil where the roots are actively growing. You should avoid wetting any soil which does not have roots actively growing in it. The soil can turn sour if it is allowed to remain wet too long.

Watering from the bottom of the pot is probably a safer way of seeing to your African violet's needs, but there are a few pitfalls to be on the lookout for when using this technique. By always adding the water to the saucer beneath the pot you will get an accumulation of fertilizer salts at the soil surface. This salty condition is seen as a white crust on the soil.

How the salt buildup occurs is quite simple. The water moves up in the soil by what is called capillary rise or, stated differently, the water is attracted to the dry soil and is pulled up into it. This in turn causes the fertilizer salts in the water and soil to accumulate at the surface.

If you continue to water your African violets from the bottom, the accumulation of these salts at the soil surface can kill your plants. To overcome this problem, water should be poured on the surface of the soil and allowed to drain out the bottom of the pot into the kitchen sink. Sufficient water should be poured through the potted soil to flush out all the accumulated salts. Pouring two to three cups of water through the soil every six weeks will keep the salt level well below the toxic level and allow normal plant growth.

When watering from the bottom, it is important that you do not keep the saucer or clay dish continually filled with water. If you do, you are guilty of overwaterring your African violets. Keeping the soil too soggy will damage the roots and cause your plants to become sickly and unsightly. Let the water stand in the dish or saucer for half an hour and then pour away the excess. This will prevent the soil from becoming soggy.

Another technique you may wish to experiment with is watering with a plant wick. Your wick may be homemade, or purchased from a garden center. Manufactured ones are usually made of spun-glass fibers; homemade ones can be coarse rope (for large pots) or a tightly rolled piece of burlap. The diameter of the wick should be approximately one-eighth inch for any pot up to four inches in diameter. Pots larger than this require an increase in the size of the wick.

USING A WICK TO WATER AFRICAN VIOLETS

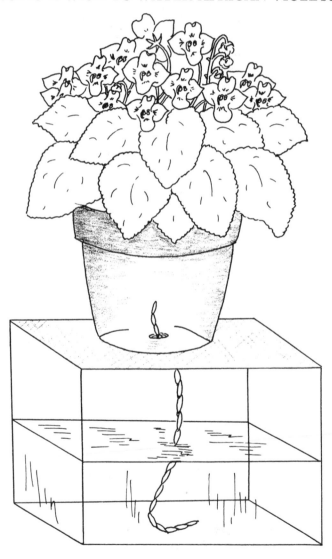

The wick should be placed in the pot at the time your African violet is potted. Fray each end of a four- to six-inch piece of the wick. After threading the wick through the drain hole, curl two or three inches up in the bottom of the pot. Next, place potting soil directly on top of the wick and gently firm the soil against the wick to insure good contact between the two. Now finish potting your African violet.

Water the plant from the top until all the soil is wet and water is dripping off the wick hanging out the drain hole. This establishes the wick action needed between the soil and the wick. Now place the potted plant above a water source and let the wick rest directly in the water. As the plant uses the moisture in the soil, the wick replenishes it.

Rewetting Dried Soil

If you should forget to water your African violets for four or five days it allows the soil in the pots to dry up and shrink in size, causing it to pull away from the sides of the pot. Pouring water in from the top is not the best way to rewet the soil, as the water will run down the inside surface of the pot and through the drain hole. This does not wet all the soil in the pot and the African violets will fail to recover completely from the drought conditions. Immediate rewetting of all the soil is important if you want the plants to be as vigorous and beautiful as they were prior to the water shortage.

Rewetting the soil is easily done by setting the pots in a pan filled with water up to the rim of the pots. The pots must have a drain hole in the bottom to rewet the soil properly using this method. Do not let the water flow over the rim into the pots. This will allow air pockets to form between the water moving up from the bottom and also draining down from the top, thus preventing some of the soil from absorbing any moisture.

After about thirty to forty-five minutes, depending on the size of the pots, the soil will be completely saturated with water. Practically all the air pockets in the soil will have been forced out as the water advanced to the surface of the potted soil. Never leave African violets immersed in the water for longer than sixty minutes. The lack of oxygen in the root zone will take its effect on the roots and kill many of them if the shortage is extended for too long a period of time.

Once the soil has become thoroughly rewetted, set the pots out on a rack and let the excess water drain away. When there isn't any more water dripping from the drain hole, use your fingers and gently push the soil firmly against the sides of the pots.

The soil now has the proper balance between water and air for healthy growth of your African violets. Return to your normal watering schedule, only this time try not to forget to give your plants their daily drink of water.

DOUBLE POTTING

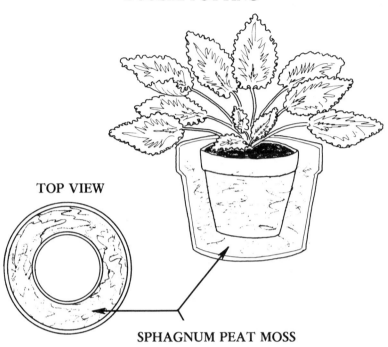

TOP VIEW

SPHAGNUM PEAT MOSS

This technique of potting plants allows them to be displayed in an attractive container while meeting their water requirements. Moist sphagnum peat moss is placed between the clay pot and the decorative container.

Potting Within a Pot

The type of pots African violets are growing in will have an effect on your watering habits. Red-clay pots are very porous and the water evaporates through them. It has been estimated that of the water poured on the soil in a clay pot, at least 50 percent of it evaporates through the sides. Glazed or fired pots are 100 percent leakproof; no water can evaporate through them.

The porosity of clay pots can be used to your advantage in a technique called double potting. This is practiced more often in large office buildings than in homes. Still, should you decide to try it, it will work just fine for you and your African violets.

The first step in double potting is to be sure that your plants are potted in a porous clay pot. After you have determined they are, then set them in a larger, decorative glazed pot. The rims of both pots should be level with one another. Fill the space between the two pots with sphagnum peat moss. Do not use one that is finely ground but choose a stringy peat moss. Dry peat moss is difficult to wet, especially after you have placed it between the pots.

A good twenty-four-hour presoaking in water prior to using it will help to overcome this.

The purpose of peat moss is to store the moisture until the plant roots are ready for it. As the roots use up the moisture the soil becomes drier in the porous pot. When this happens, the moisture from peat moss moves through the porous pot sides and replenishes the moisture in the soil. All you need to remember is to keep the peat moss damp, and the African violets will have a steady source of moisture. This will allow you to water them less frequently than when you grow them in single pots.

Double potting is especially adapted to those places in your home where there are low light intensities. Under this situation African violets require less water, so this method gives them the moisture more uniformly and in correct proportion to their needs. Thus you eliminate the tendency to over-water plants grown under these circumstances.

Now you are ready to move your newly potted African violets to a prominent spot in your home. Double potting allows you to have your African violets in attractive decorative pots that enhance their natural beauty.

Vacation Watering

Many fine African violet collections have been drastically reduce when their owners left for a vacation or even a short four- or five-day business trip. Death of the plants is usually attributed to a lack of moisture under these conditions. Thirsty plants don't last long. Once they begin to wilt, it is only a matter of hours before it is too late to save them. Whether you are only going to be away for a few days or a couple of weeks, make arrangements to have a friend look in on your African violets and see to their needs.

There are a few things you can do to insure that the plants will be okay when you return. If you are just going to be out of town for two or three days, why not build a miniature greenhouse around your plants? Sounds complicated, but in fact it is very simple. Place each potted plant inside a clear plastic bag and tie the bag at the top about twelve to fourteen inches above the plant. Use a long stick pushed into the soil to hold the plastic up and away from the plant. Three sticks in a triangular formation work ideally. Do not allow any direct sunlight to fall on the plants when they are enclosed in this tent-like greenhouse, for it will bake them in a few short hours.

You may wish to snip off all the flowers and developing buds before you cover the plants with plastic. As these plant parts become mature and start to die they easily become infected with disease, especially when the air is going to be as moist as it is inside the bag.

Be sure to water the plants thoroughly before you enclose them in the miniature greenhouses. The purpose of all this is to create an ideal growing chamber where the humidity is kept very high due to water evaporation. Water consumption is thus reduced and allows the African violets to go several days before they use up the available water supply.

Place each African violet in a miniature greenhouse while you are away on vacation. This will help conserve soil moisture, allowing the plants to go longer between waterings.

If you plan to be away from home for more than just a few days, you should prepare your plants for your absence by conditioning them to survive periods of drought. African violets can go for as long as two weeks if they have been readied for the ordeal. Prepare your African violets by subjecting them to droughty conditions over a four- to eight-week period just prior to your departure. By letting the plants reach the wilting stage on several occasions, they will become accustomed to having less water and will adapt to these new growing conditions.

If possible, place all the plants in a room where the temperature is around 65 degrees F., and the light intensities are very low (but not complete darkness). By doing this you will slow down the growth of the plants and thus reduce the amount of water needed by them for their daily requirements.

Going on vacation and leaving your African violets to make it on their own after taking these steps is still risky business. I would reserve this method as a last resort for use when all your relatives, close friends, and neighbors will be away at the same time you are.

You still have one other choice that is by far the best way of seeing to your African violets' needs while you and your family are enjoying the beach or hiking in the mountains. The self-watering wick technique, which has already been discussed, provides a suitable means of watering the plants. Take the spun-glass, thread-like wicks and firmly press one end into the potted soil. Let the other end hang down into a bowl or glass of water. As the soil dries out, the water is pulled up through the wick to replenish the plant's water supply. This will keep the soil moderately moist all the time.

Using a wick to water African violets works fine, unless your water reserve is used up or it completely evaporates from the bowl before your return. Allow for enough water storage in whatever type container you use to last your entire trip.

Even when using this simple technique, I would still recommend having a friend look in on your plants at least once a week. Your plants are too valuable to just leave for two or more weeks and assume that their watering needs have been taken care of. A happy vacation time can have a sad ending if you return to a houseful of African violets which have died.

Another thing to remember while on vacation if a friend is looking after your plants: the pots should be turned once a week. This will expose different sides of the plants to the light and help them to grow evenly and remain symmetrical.

Mixing Water and Plant Food

The subject of plant food is covered in Chapter 5. If you wish more detailed information on plant fertilizers, refer to that chapter. It explains the what, when and how of feeding African violets. Here I plan to look briefly at one specific way of giving African violets the food they need.

A wide variety of packaged plant foods are available on counters in every garden center. Even the nationwide department-store chains carry plant supplies. It's big business. There are several different kinds of plant foods from which to choose. Many will even be labeled as specially formulated for African violets. Select one which gives the amount to be mixed with water so you can prepare the correct mixture. Getting the proper amount of fertilizer dissolved in water is important. It is easy to get it too concentrated and burn the roots when the mixture is applied. Follow the directions; if it calls for one-and-one-quarter teaspoons per gallon of water, do not add an extra three-quarters of a teaspoon for good measure. Approximately every two to three weeks, water with the fertilizer-water combination.

This mixture should be applied to the soil surface. The plant food will work its way down into the soil where the roots are. Letting it soak in from the bottom causes the fertilizer salts to accumulate on the surface of the soil and forms a white crust. This salt, if allowed to come in contact with the leaves or petioles will cause them to rot. Periodically pouring water (two or three cups) through the soil from the top will wash some of the excess fertilizer salts from the soil. Let the water go down the drain. Never reuse it.

Bathing Your African Violets

Dust from the air settles on the leaves of your African violets at an alarming rate. Just consider how many times a week you must dust your furniture, and you can readily visualize the problem of dust on your plants.

There are two problems dust causes when it begins to accumulate on the leaves. As this dust collects on the plants, it reduces the efficiency of the photosynthesis factories located in the leaves. When this happens, the food supply is drastically reduced and both growth and flowering are affected. It is important to the health of your African violets to keep the dust off them.

Use a soft brush to gently sweep the dust off of the plant leaves. Dust ruins the plant's beauty and reduces the amount of light the leaves can absorb.

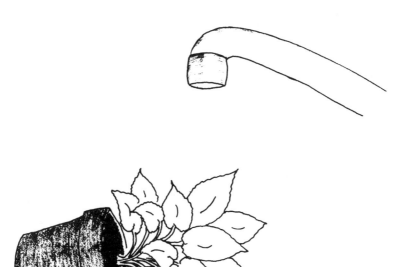

Dusty leaves will reduce a plant's ability to produce flowers for your enjoyment. Periodically wash the leaves under a faucet. Temperature of the water should be carefully regulated to prevent damage to the plant.

The other problem, although not quite as serious, is still an important consideration to keep in mind if you are proud of your African violets and plan to display them in your home. The appearance of your plants can be ruined if you let too much dust and grime collect on them. The leaves will turn from a beautiful deep green to a dingy grayish color.

To avoid a dust buildup on your plants, buy a soft, half-inch wide, camel's hair brush. Use this brush like a broom to remove dust from the leaves. Be ever so gentle when brushing the leaves so as not to damage any of them. You should try to brush the plant leaves at least once a week to keep them looking healthy and attractive.

Do not use a stiff-bristled brush to remove dust. It will damage the sensitive foilage and leave unsightly blemishes and bruises on the delicate flowers if you are careless.

Another way of removing the dust is to wash it off with a warm mist spray or under the kitchen tap. The water should be at room temperature and free of chlorine, if possible. Also it is a good idea to check the water temperature prior to spraying it on your African violets. The use of water with a temperature variance of 10 degrees either way from room temperature will also be harmful to your plants.

Keep a thermometer close to your plants so you know what the temperature is where they are living. Have another one handy for testing the temperature of the water prior to bathing your plants. Remember, a 10 degree difference is all it takes to turn healthy plants into sickly ones.

When washing the leaves, hold the plant so that the water drips off into the sink. Avoid getting too much water in the pot, especially if the crown of the plant is getting wet. There is always the possibility of crown-rot disease anytime an African violet gets too wet.

Let the plants dry off in a location where direct sunlight will not reach them. As earlier mentioned, exposing wet leaves to direct sunlight will cause burned spots. Once the plants have dried off, it is safe to move them back into moderate to bright light intensities.

Never use leaf-cleaning or shining compounds, liquid or spray, on African violets. The hairy leaves are not adapted for these preparations. Either a camel's hair brush or plain water are still best for cleaning your plants.

4

Environmental Factors: Temperature, Light, Humidity, and Air Movement

*T*he living conditions in your home have a definite effect on your African violets. Although they are capable of adjusting to your life style, there are limits as to how far they can rearrange their growing habits. Evaluate the various locations in your home where you would like to show off your elegant African violets, and then pick the spots best suited to their lifestyle.

Temperature, humidity, air movement, and light are the big four environmental conditions in which plants must learn to live. Temperature and light are the two most important environmental factors; air movement and humidity tend to be given second billing. The latter two are important to the well-being of your plants and should not be overlooked.

Intensity or brightness of light falling on African violets plays a major role in how well they perform for you. If you do not give the plants a proper amount of light every day, they will suffer from your neglect. Proper lighting is so important for growing healthy African violets that I have devoted three chapters to this subject. One chapter deals with how plants use the light in their growth; another covers the use of artificial lighting for improving the flowering and appearance of African violets, and the third chapter tells you about the care plants need when you grow them under artificial lights.

Temperature Requirements

African violets have been found growing under a wide range of temperatures in nature. Some were found doing exceptionally well at

59

temperatures as low as 40 degrees F. and others at 90 degrees F. Your African violets won't survive long if you subject them to such temperatures. The plants developed for indoor use have been those which are adapted to the temperatures you are comfortable with in your home.

Temperature Ranges for Growing African Violets

Ideally the best temperatures for healthy African violets and vigorous growth vary slightly from daytime to nighttime. If you can, locate your plants where daytime temperatures are between 70 and 75 degrees F., and nighttime temperatures range from 60 to 65 degrees F.

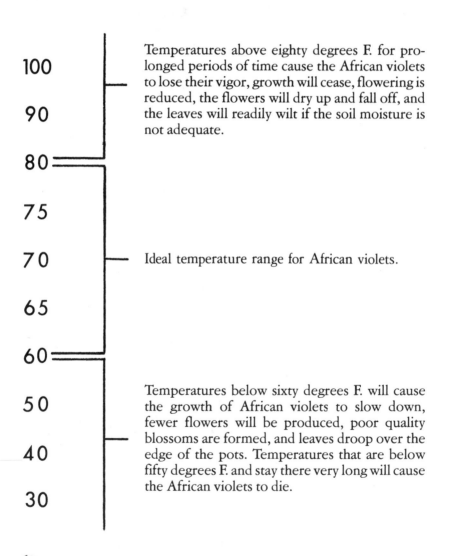

100
90
80

Temperatures above eighty degrees F. for prolonged periods of time cause the African violets to lose their vigor, growth will cease, flowering is reduced, the flowers will dry up and fall off, and the leaves will readily wilt if the soil moisture is not adequate.

75

70

Ideal temperature range for African violets.

65

60
50
40
30

Temperatures below sixty degrees F. will cause the growth of African violets to slow down, fewer flowers will be produced, poor quality blossoms are formed, and leaves droop over the edge of the pots. Temperatures that are below fifty degrees F. and stay there very long will cause the African violets to die.

To completely control temperatures around your plants would require growing them in a greenhouse. More realistically, aim for an overall temperature range of 60 to 80 degrees F. throughout day and night. The extra margin in temperature at either end of the range may put a little stress on the African violets. If you make a special point to look after all the other plant care needs, your plants will not show any ill effects caused by temperatures in which they are required to live.

Temperature Extremes Cause Problems

When temperatures become higher or lower than the 60 to 80 degrees F. where your African violets will perform as expected, the overall quality of the plants is reduced. High temperatures do not cause as many problems as lower temperatures. When the thermometer moves above 80 toward 90 degrees F. plants react by refusing to produce flowers. Also their vigor sharply declines. The plants will withstand these high temperatures if there is an adequate supply of water available. Since you are undoubtedly interested in healthy plants with masses of flowers adorning them, do not let high temperatures persist for too long. Move the plants to a cooler spot.

At the other end of the scale you can easily lose your African violet collection if you let the temperatures drop too low. When your plants are exposed to 50 to 60 degree F. temperatures for a prolonged time, new flower buds and the flowers will be damaged. They have a very delicate cellular structure which does not react well to cool temperatures. It is a distinct possibility that they will die at these low temperatures.

If the temperature drops below 50 degrees F. the entire plant may give up the struggle and die. At these lower temperatures a disease called crown rot is very likely to attack the plants, and within a few short days all the leaves will wilt and one by one slowly drop off. At this point the only thing you can do is toss the plant into the garbage and vow to take better care of the rest of your African violets.

Avoid Chilling Your Plants

Many African violet hobbyists move their plants into windowsills during the warmer summer months. North windows are especially adapted to this practice because the amount of light reaching the plants is ideal. But as fall approaches and the evenings begin cooling off, you need to be aware of temperature changes that occur on those windowsills. Remember that the temperature on the north side of a house will be cooler than on the south side.

In early fall, when temperatures are hovering at the dangerous point, have a thermometer on the windowsill. Check it frequently and, if necessary, have some pieces of cardboard you can place between the windows and the plants. The cardboard will act as an insulation barrier and allow you to keep the plants on the windowsills for several weeks longer. Don't press your luck. When daytime temperatures begin to drop early in the afternoon it is time to move your plants to a warmer, more secure place.

There are two other points to remember when growing African violets on a windowsill. Often the leaves will be touching the panes of glass in the window. Glass is an excellent conductor of heat and cold. Any leaves in contact with the glass can be easily damaged by quick temperature changes outside. This is especially true for sudden drops in temperature in spring and fall.

There is a tendency to open the windows in a home to let in fresh air. This practice can cause problems for your plants if they are on the sill of one of the open windows or nearby. If a sudden chilling draft begins blowing through the windows on the African violets, you should move them or close the windows. African violets are very sensitive to these chilling drafts and are quickly damaged if not protected from them.

Drafts may also occur when you have your African violets near an outside door. When you or your children are frequently going in and out the door, drafts can affect the plants. Check the location of your plants to the outside doors in your home to determine if any cool drafts will reach them.

If you have forgotten about your African violets and accidentally exposed them to chilling temperatures on a windowsill (or anywhere else) you will know within thirty-six hours how well the plants have taken it. If the temperature drop was severe enough the entire plant, or maybe only parts of it, will turn a darker color and take on the characteristic water-soaked or translucent look. This is quickly followed by wilting and then death.

When only parts of a plant have died but the appearance of the plant is ruined, don't toss away the entire plant. Snip off any remaining leaves and begin propagating a whole new bunch of plants. You can turn a near-disaster into a household of your favorite African violets in five to eight months from leaf cuttings.

Reversing Day and Night Temperatures

It has been shown by researchers that if the temperature requirements of African violets are reversed the plants will actually flower a little better. This would mean that nighttime temperatures were actually a little warmer than those of daytime.

Reversing the temperature from the way it occurs in nature is relatively simple. All you need is a room where you can control the temperature with a thermostat or by opening and closing vents in the room. Basements lend themselves well to changing a temperature cycle. Another possibility is building a miniature greenhouse. Plan on using artificial lighting if you grow your plants in the basement. Without sufficient lighting African violets will fail to produce any flowers. If you have never grown plants under artificial lighting, refer to the last three chapters of this book. Growing plants under lights is a fascinating and rewarding hobby you may wish to try elsewhere in your home.

Humidity Important To African Violets

When discussing the relative humidity of the air we are talking about the percentage of moisture present in the air. It can vary considerably from day to day. The area where you live also has a bearing on the relative humidity. The arid western states have very little moisture in the air; while in the midwest, deep south, and along the east coast, the humidity is often very high.

Measurement of relative humidity and the complicated conditions which govern the amount of moisture air can hold is all very interesting, but let's leave this phase of the weather to the weatherman. You can buy simple gauges at almost any hardware or department store that will show you the relative humidity. These gauges always read in percent of the moisture present in the air.

The relative humidity plays an important role in the overall health and well-being of your African violets. Originally they were found growing in the moist, highly humid, tropical areas of Africa where the humidity remains an almost constant 90 percent.

In your home it is impossible to have the humidity as high as it gets in the tropics. The farther north you live, and in the arid regions of the country, the percent of moisture held in the air also lessens during the winter months. The warmer air of summer is capable of holding more moisture than the cooler winter air.

Fortunately African violets can be kept happy at a humidity level much below the 90 percent the native plants are used to. African violets will do well anytime local humidity has dropped as low as 40 to 50 percent. They will really thrive when you are able to get the moisture as high as 50 to 70 percent. Anytime you achieve these higher percentages and are able to maintain them for an extended time, you will be rewarded with some very beautiful African violet plants.

Before looking into some of the ways you can increase the humidity around your plants, let's see what effect too low a relative humidity does to them. The African violet's overall growth is not as vigorous in low humidity. More important, the flowering of the plants is reduced and thus affects the most important reason why you are growing them. Although the vegetation of African violets is pretty, their crowning glory is the bouquet of blossoms which adorns them.

If the humidity is allowed to remain low for too long the plants will need plenty of time to completely recover from the ill effects. With proper attention and plenty of patience your African violets will return to their natural beauty.

Humidity in the home can be manipulated in various ways. Remember that you are interested only in the humidity directly around your plants. If you try to raise the humidity in your entire home to meet the needs of the plants, you will be waging an unnecessary battle.

63

Several highly humid areas of your home offer natural spots for growing African violets. The kitchen and bathroom are two locations where water is often used. As the water evaporates, the humidity increases in these areas. Another spot to consider because of humid conditions is the basement of your home. The cool moist air tends to accumulate here.

You can affect the humidity around your plants by the way you group them. The humidity will naturally be higher around a bunch of potted plants than around a single one. However, you must be careful in grouping your African violet plants. Maintain good ventilation or air circulation around the plants. A few loosely grouped plants is fine. African violets packed in too small an area (leaves touching each other) will very often lose their vigor and become spindly. The importance of good air circulation around your plants is discussed next in this chapter.

One of the best ways to increase the humidity is to fill a pan with sand, pea gravel, vermiculite or sphagnum peat moss, and place it among your plants. Keep the material in the pan continually damp, and as the moisture evaporates it will raise the humidity around the plants.

Three simple ways of increasing the humidity around your plants are shown here. Remember, African violets were originally found growing in steaming tropical valleys where the humidity is always seventy to ninety percent. High humidity causes these lovely plants to be prolific bloomers.

Plants sitting on moist pebbles in a tray.

Misting the leaves.

Containers of water sitting among the plants.

You may consider buying a humidifier for your forced-air furnace to add moisture during the winter months. This not only works for the well-being of the plants, but for your family as well. A 35 percent relative humidity level should be minimal, but this is still short of the 40 to 50 percent humidity African violets desire. Plan on using one of the other methods discussed in conjunction with the furnace humidifier to raise the humidity directly around the plants.

65

Misting the plants is an excellent technique to use on the humidity-loving African violets. Buy yourself a small hand mister or atomizer, and every two days spray a fine mist over your plants. They'll love it. This fine misting works wonders, but don't overdo it. If you spray too much moisture on the leaves and allow it to accumulate and run down on the crown of the plant you will have problems. Excess moisture may allow crown-rot disease to set in which could kill your plants.

You have read about the various ways to influence the relative humidity to create a better home for your African violets. Now go out and buy yourself a guage to check the humidity around your plants. If it is too low, get busy and do something about it.

Air Movement

Just as you enjoy the feeling of fresh air on your skin so do the leaves of the African violets. Stale, stagnant air does not allow plants to reach their full potential. They need a steady supply of fresh air, gently circulating around their leaves to obtain the peak of perfection you expect of them.

Crowding too many plants into a small area is a mistake. I realize you want as many of these beautiful plants around the house as possible, but confining them to a small area reduces the air movement around each individual plant. When this happens they become sickly and fail to produce the flowers you are so eagerly awaiting.

When trying to insure good air circulation around your plants remember that directed air movement can be harmful to them. This is especially true if it is a very forceful air current and colder than the room where the plants are growing.

Basements and rooms which are frequently closed up most of the time will have inadequate air circulation. Small electric fans with a six to eight-inch diameter can be used to increase the air flow around your African violets. Be sure to set the fans at the slowest possible speed. Do not aim the fans directly at the plants but slightly above them. The fan should be located far enough away from the plants to create a very soft, gentle breeze.

An African violet in full blossom makes a lovely accent piece or even a striking focal point of interest in a room. When you use a plant for this purpose you need not worry about air movement around the plant. A room where people are moving about throughout the day has adequate air circulation.

Just why is good air circulation around African violets so important? You know it has something to do with the overall health of your plants and that it affects their flowering, but let's delve a little deeper into how a plant operates at the cellular level and what its basic needs are.

Carbon dioxide is one of the main ingredients which must be present in plant leaves in order for photosynthesis to occur. By a series of very complicated chemical reactions the carbon dioxide is converted into the energy (sugars and other carbohydrates) plants need for their growth. Without this carbon dioxide plants cannot continue to grow and would die if the supply were cut off completely. To humans, carbon dioxide is a pollutant and of little direct use. Our atmosphere contains about 300 to 500 ppm (parts per million) of carbon dioxide. This is lower than plants would like to have it. However, out-of-doors there is good enough air movement to keep plants continuously resupplied with sufficient quantities of carbon dioxide. Indoors where your African violets are growing is a different story.

Usually there is less air movement around the leaves of an indoor plant. This means that as the plant absorbs carbon dioxide there is a zone around the plant which has a lower concentration of carbon dioxide present. Fortunately the overall amount of carbon dioxide in your home is higher than in the air outside. You inhale oxygen and exhale carbon dioxide, thus increasing its concentration to 500 to 600 ppm. By improving the air circulation around plants you are moving a fresh supply of carbon dioxide to the plants, making more available for the photosynthetic process. The end result is a very vigorous, healthy African violet.

Carbon dioxide levels are not something you need to become concerned over. Don't go out and buy some gadget to measure the levels of carbon dioxide in your home. Nature has taken good care of everything for you.

5

Feeding Your African Violets

*T*he first recorded use of a fertilizer to stimulate plant growth was written by a fellow by the name of Homer. Around 900 to 700 B.C. he told of his father using animal manure to improve his vineyards. In 400 B.C. Roman farmers had actually rated the various kinds of manure as to which one was the best for crop production.

Today we have become very scientific with fertilizers and their application. To be a successful African violet grower it helps to understand how fertilizers actually help the plants produce those lovely blossoms. Part of the enjoyment of growing African violets or doing any kind of gardening is understanding what you are doing, and using this knowledge to help friends solve their problems.

All green plants have the same plant foods to choose from for their diets. Regardless of what you give them or what is already in the soil, plants will use only sixteen different types of plant food. These are referred to as "the sixteen essential plant nutrients." If you are giving your African violets excellent care yet they lack the vigor you think they should have, consider the possibility that one or all of these essential nutrients aren't being fed to them. You may be starving them to death.

The ways in which the nutrients are utilized by a plant will vary. Some will enter through the leaves of the plant; others are absorbed by the roots. In some cases the nutrients will enter through both leaves and roots, depending on how you prepared them before applying them.

You do not need to become an expert on plant fertilizers, but it is always fun to know a little more than your friends do about growing plants. After all, some day you may be able to use the information to help them, making you the expert and them the students.

Just keep in mind that a well-fed plant is a healthy one, and so it is up to you to keep it supplied and happy. The fertilizer is your tool to complete this job.

Keep a permanent record of when you fertilize your African violets. It is awfully easy to forget when you have last fed your plants and what you gave

68

them. Have a calendar handy and write on it each time you feed the plants. This same calendar can be used for recording any other information you wish to remember about your African violets. For example, if you place a new cutting in water, make a note on the calendar; then when the roots begin to develop you can check to find out how long it took.

Another handy record-keeping technique is to use 3″ x 5″ cards and store them in a recipe box. If you have several African violets, make a card for each one and record your observations on how they are doing.

Knowing your plants is important. Each has its own individual personality. Working closely with them and observing how they grow will help in planning their diet. Some of the plants will be fast growers; other may be slow and easygoing. Don't try to force these slow growers or you'll just be creating problems for yourself.

Nutrients Needed by Plants

You have already read that there are sixteen essential nutrients a plant must have in order to survive. African violets are no exception. Here is a list of those plant foods:

Nitrogen	Molybdenum
Phosphorus	Chlorine
Potassium	Oxygen
Calcium	Carbon
Magnesium	Hydrogen
Sulfur	Iron
Copper	Boron
Zinc	Manganese

The amount of each of these nutrients needed by plants will vary. Those needed in large amounts are called major nutrients (nitrogen, phosphorus, and potassium); others needed only in moderate quantities are referred to as secondary nutrients (calcium, magnesium and sulfur); and those plant food elements needed in very small amounts are called trace nutrients (iron, boron, zinc, chlorine, copper, manganese and molybdenum). The three remaining nutrients (oxygen, hydrogen and carbon) are not categorized since the plants obtain them from air and water.

The breakdown of plant nutrients into these three categories does not mean that any one group is more important to the plant than the others. If any one of these nutrients is withheld from your plants for a long enough time they would die. These categories serve only to remind you of the approximate amount needed by the plants.

I have heard experienced African violet growers talk about the vitamins and proteins they give their plants, and how they feed their plants over thirty different plant nutrients which are absolutely essential to the health of their

African violets. There are mixtures on the market which do claim to contain these special ingredients, and they probably do. But your plants will use only those sixteen present on the preceding list. You can speak with authority anytime you want to state the exact number of nutrients needed by your African violets. Chances are you'll not get many opportunities, but at least you'll be absolutely correct when you do.

Purpose of Each Nutrient

Let's briefly run through the different plant nutrients and find out exactly what role each one plays in the life of an African violet. Once you become acquainted with them, you'll have a better appreciation of the importance of properly feeding your African violets.

Nitrogen

The role this plant food plays is very important. Nitrogen is one of the building blocks of the chlorophyll molecule contained in all green plants. You can say it causes plants to be green, because if nitrogen is absent the leaves lose their color and turn yellow.

Protoplasm (cell sap) contains proteins, amino acids, and many other important plant compounds, all of which must have nitrogen in their makeup in order to be of use to the plant. Nitrogen must be thought of as one of the primary ingredients for a healthy African violet.

Phosphorus

Almost as versatile as nitrogen, this plant food is the key to many important plant functions. Its presence will insure good root growth, flowering of your plants, and it also promotes plant development and strong stems. Compounds within the plant cells that give off the energy for a plant to do all these things must have phosphorus in them.

Potassium

"Always on the move" is probably the best way to describe this nutrient's status in a plant. Its exact function isn't known; but if it is missing, the plant's reaction can be easily predicted. It has been credited with making plants more resistant to diseases, causing the plants to be able to withstand cooler temperatures than normal, and aiding plant roots by improving their ability to absorb other plant nutrients from the soil.

Calcium

Cementing of the plant's cells to one another is calcium's role in the plant. Just as nitrogen is a major building block in the plant, the strength of calcium is what holds the plant kingdom together. The roots must have a good supply of this particular plant food.

Magnesium

If any one nutrient could be referred to as "the heart" of a plant, magnesium would surely qualify for the honor. Each chlorophyll molecule in a plant is composed of two identical parts, with magnesium in the center holding the parts together to form the chlorophyll molecule.

Sulfur

Very seldom does this nutrient receive mention, yet a plant contains three times more sulfur than the combined total of phosphorus, calcium, and magnesium. African violets use sulfur in a wide variety of ways. It joins up with nitrogen in the chlorophyll molecule, aids in production of cell sap, and helps to speed up many plant-growing processes.

Iron

Iron is often found in large quantities in the soil mixture but in a form that plant roots cannot use. This particular plant food works in close association with nitrogen and sulfur and aids them in the formation of the chlorophyll molecule.

Boron

Only a very small quantity of boron is needed by African violets. If you were to scientifically test your plants and find six to eight parts per million of boron present in them, this would be ideal. Water uptake by the roots is aided by the presence of boron in the plant. Somehow boron assists the plant's defense mechanism which prevents a large amount of the absorbed water from evaporating and escaping from the plant back into the atmosphere.

Manganese

Like boron, very small amounts of this nutrient will allow it to perform its three functions in a plant. It aids in the formation of the chlorophyll molecule, makes other plant foods more accessible to the plant, and causes germination to occur quickly when propagating African violets from seed.

Copper

Scientists believe that copper plays a role in the way that chlorophyll molecules react when light strikes them. Copper also acts as an energizer (activates enzymes) for starting several important plant processes which produce healthy plants.

Zinc, Molybdenum, and Chlorine

The role of these three nutrients isn't completely known. In fact, about all that is known about chlorine is that its presence is necessary for the growth of your plants. Zinc and molybdenum are activating compounds which cause certain plant-growing processes to occur.

Very seldom will you need to concern yourself with the trace nutrients (iron, boron, manganese, copper, zinc, molybdenum, or chlorine). Small quantities of these plant nutrients are present in most fertilizers you use, plus the soil mixture your plants are growing in releases these nutrients for the plant's use.

Types of Plant Food

When you are ready to buy plant food for your African violets you need to understand the information given on the container. Laws govern what the manufacturers must put on their labels, so you will not be shortchanged if you read the label. Primarily you are interested in the total amount of plant food present and the proportion of nutrients to each other.

Every bag, bottle, or box must have the percentage of nitrogen, phosphorus, and potassium shown on the label, if any is present. These three percentages are called the ''grade'' of the fertilizer. It is important that you look for these percentages when buying a fertilizer because they play a major role in how well your African violets grow.

Use these three percentages to determine how much of the material in the container is actually plant food. For example, if the container is listed as having 10 percent nitrogen, 20 percent phosphorous, and 20 percent potassium (shown on the container as follows: 10-20-20) and weighs 16 ounces, you have 8 ounces of plant food present. You simply add the percentages and multiply them times the weight (50 percent x 16 ounces = 8 ounces of plant food) to come up with the answer. The other 8 ounces of material found in the container is of no value to the plants; it merely acts as a carrier to allow even distribution of the fertilizer.

The ratio of the nitrogen, phosphorus, and potassium contained in a fertilizer will influence the growth of African violets. A plant food high in nitrogen and low in phosphorus and potassium will stimulate the plant leaves to grow and become a deep-green color, but flowering is suppressed. Select this type fertilizer for young plants which have just been rooted and need to grow and mature before they are able to produce flowers. Examples of fertilizers to use for this purpose would be: 30-10-10 or 10-4-4.

After the plants are mature and flowering, cut back on the nitrogen you give them and supply more phosphorus and potassium. Something like 10-30-20 or 5-10-10 would promote flowering and give the plant enough nitrogen for a healthy appearance.

Occasionally you will see some of the other plant nutrients listed on fertilizer boxes. This is done occasionally when a manufacturer wants to make the product look a little better than the others on the shelves.

Be primarily interested in the percentages of nitrogen, phosphorus, and potassium. Anything else just adds to the overall cost of the fertilizer. Fortunately when the basic fertilizers are mixed, the secondary and trace nutrients tend to be present in sufficient amounts to keep your African violets happy. These nutrients are also naturally found in the soil mix you use for your plants.

Natural Organic Versus Manufactured Plant Foods

If you have ever spent an evening with plant growers who do all their gardening using the "organic method," I am sure you have been told that you should never use chemically manufactured plant food. They claim that manufactured fertilizers are not good for you or for your plants. Manures, compost material, or any product produced by nature is the only way to feed plants—according to the organic gardeners.

If these gardeners are successful using only naturally formed organic fertilizers, good for them. But their claim of commercially boxed, chemically manufactured fertilizers being harmful to plants is inaccurate. Go ahead and use them on your African violets without fear of damaging your plants—so long as you follow the directions on the label.

Before a plant can utilize any plant food it has to be absorbed by the roots or sometimes through the leaves. In order for the plant to do this, each individual plant nutrient must be in its most basic or elemental form. This means that no matter what kind of material is used, organic or chemical, it all has to break down to the simple forms to be taken into the plant.

The fibers or organic matter of compost or manure must decompose and release the nitrogen in the nitrate form for the plant to use. The same is true for the nitrogen contained in chemical fertilizer. The only difference is that it takes much longer for organic material to release the nitrogen.

This controversy over organic versus chemical fertilizers is one over which you needn't be too concerned. But if you ever run into organic gardeners who want to convert everyone to their gardening methods, stand your ground. They will have several valid-sounding arguments for their way of growing plants, but it all narrows down to just exactly how the plant absorbs the nutrients. Regardless of the type material used, it is all the same to the plants.

Ways to Apply Your Fertilizer

It doesn't matter to the African violet how you feed it. So long as you do not use too much fertilizer you can't really go wrong. The amount and frequency of application of plant food will be discussed in a few paragraphs.

There are three basic ways to apply a fertilizer once the plants have been potted. One method is to put the fertilizer granules or pellets on the soil mixture and let the water slowly dissolve them. The other two ways deal

THREE WAYS TO FEED YOUR PLANTS

Carefully measure a granular fertilizer and pour it onto the soil of the potted plants.

Dissolve the plant food in water and feed your African violets as you water them.

74

Dissolve the fertilizer in water and spray the solution onto the leaves of the plants.

with dissolving the fertilizer in water and either pouring the solution on the soil, or spraying it on the plant leaves.

If I were asked to rate these three methods as to which is best, I would prefer pouring the fertilizer solution onto the soil mixture. Spreading the granular material on the soil would be next, and last place would go to the foliar feeding technique. Most African violet fertilizers available are designed for use either by my first or second choice. The amount you use will be given on the container. Follow the directions carefully.

Foliar feeding has been tried by several different researchers with varying degrees of success. Some have found that almost all the fertilizer was absorbed very quickly through the leaves of the African violets. Others caution against using this method of fertilizing your plants because you may actually harm them.

If you wish to try foliar feeding, I would suggest that you limit your endeavors to one or two plants until you can personally judge the results. Why take the chance of damaging all your African violets until you know what to expect. Pick out a plant that is not growing as well as the others. The leaves should be smaller, yellowish in color. If after spraying the plant with a foliar solution it perks up, the leaves turn green, and the overall appearance improves, you will have your answer.

Foliar feeding, if you are successful, should be limited for use as a quick way to pull a plant out of a sickly state. It is best to do most of your fertilizing so the roots can absorb the nutrients supplied to the plant.

How Often Should You Fertilize?

When trying to decide when to fertilize your African violets keep in mind how fast they are growing, whether they are flowering, and the time of the year. All these things should enter the picture as you are making your decision. Once you set a regular feeding schedule your plants will almost tell you when they are hungry.

Actively growing plants use up certain plant nutrients much more quickly than others. These nutrients (nitrogen and potassium) are used in larger amounts by plants and they also easily leach out of the bottom of the pot. This is why these two plant foods should be present in all fertilizers you select for your African violets.

Most people tend to put too much fertilizer on their plants. Feeding plants once or twice a week to force growth and more flowers can be disastrous. The question of how often to fertilize your plants is not an easy one to answer directly. There are a lot of "ifs" and "buts" to be taken into consideration. If your plant is healthy and growing well then there is no need to feed it and force it to grow any more. But on the other hand, you don't want to wait too long and let a healthy plant start downhill before the next application of fertilizer.

How often, then, should you fertilize your African violets? The guidelines laid out in the next few paragraphs will answer this question for you. Newly propagated young plants getting a good start after potting need a fairly constant food supply. After potting, wait about a month before fertilizing them. Start feeding them at seven-to-ten-day intervals for the next four to six months. About the time they are mature enough to begin flowering, switch over to feeding them once a month.

Mature African violets which are actively producing flowers should be fed once a month. Resting plants that have temporarily stopped flowering should not be fertilized in an attempt to force them to start flowering. Give them a break. When they naturally begin to flower again, start back on a regular feeding program.

Occasionally your mature plants may just quit growing for no apparent reason; when this happens, check your calendar record to see if you missed a feeding. Chances are you did.

Usually you can skip winter feeding of your plants. The light intensity is very low and the day length so short that growth has been reduced. An exception to this is if you are growing the plants under artificial lights, such as fluorescent tubes.

Summer, spring, and fall, when both the day length and light intensity are excellent for growing African violets, you need to be on a sound fertilization program. Watch your plants closely; their appearance and rate of growth will tell you when to feed them. Sometimes African violets look terrific but some of the lower, older leaves are sort of light-green to yellowish in color. Don't just snip them off thinking that old age has set in on these leaves. Anytime plant leaves begin looking yellowish it is safe to assume that the nitrogen level is too low. Try adding a little nitrogen to the soil; the leaves might green up again in a week's time. Overapplication of nitrogen can be fatal too, so be careful and add only a very small amount.

When to fertilize a newly repotted plant will depend on how good a job you did in handling the plant and its soil ball. If the soil was not knocked loose and the roots weren't disturbed in the transfer from one pot to another, you can safely fertilize in a week to ten days. A plant whose soil ball was broken and exposed the roots should not be fertilized until the plant has a chance to recover from shock and starts growing again. This will be in about four weeks.

The way you are watering your African violets has some influence on

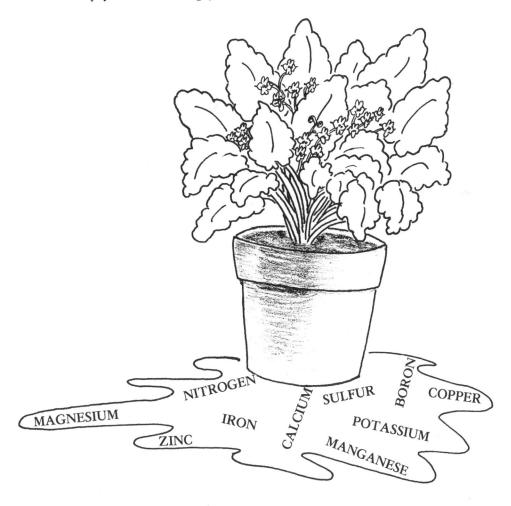

Top watering prevents the build-up of salts in the soil, but it also washes the plant food out of the soilball. Do not reuse this water. Plan on feeding the plants often enough to replace the plant food lost through the drain hole.

your fertilizer program. As previously mentioned, whenever you top-water a plant there is a tendency to wash the plant nutrients out the bottom of the pot. Deletion of these nutrients from the soil will affect the frequency with which you feed your African violets.

Bottom watering also influences the feeding program. The fertilizer salts will accumulate at the soil surface and form a white crust. In such a case fertilize less to reduce the amount of fertilizer salts present in the soil. The idea is to apply the fertilizer at about the same rate the roots are absorbing it. This way there is less chance of accumulating salts in the soil.

SALT BUILD-UP

Salt accumulation distracts from the appearance of any plant grown in this pot. African violets will develop petiole rot if the leaf comes into contact with the salt on the rim of the pot.

One final point needs to be touched on before moving on to the next topic. Be sure that the soil is already wet before adding your fertilizer to the pot. Fertilizer salts can damage African violet roots if applied when the soil is dry. A wet soil will also allow the roots to absorb the nutrients more easily and give the plant a quick boost.

How Much to Apply

I'll not go into how much plant food to mix in a gallon of water to make up a fertilizer solution, or how many ounces or teaspoons of granular plant food to give your African violets. Specific amounts will vary according to the percent of nitrogen, phosphorus, and potassium present in the fertilizer.

Read the label on the fertilizer container; it will tell you exactly how much is needed for a proper fertilizer mixture. Follow the directions and you will be okay. Remembering the age of the plant and whether it is flowering will determine what type (grade) of fertilizer you choose.

A safe practice to follow when using plant food is to use less than the recommended amount. This will reduce the chances of damaging any of the delicate roots and lower the salt level in the soil mixture. By cutting the recommended rate by exactly half, the plant will be able to absorb most of the nutrients between the intervals you apply them.

Incorporation of fertilizer into soil mixtures prior to potting your African violets should be mentioned here also. If you are to have healthy plants, their roots must be set in a rich soilbed to get them off to a good start. You won't be adding any fertilizer for a month after potting them, so you need to mix in some plant food with the mixture when you prepare it.

Be careful not to add too much fertilizer to the soil mixture, for the high concentration of fertilizer salts will damage the plant's roots. The percentage of plant food will tell you how much to add. The higher the total precentage of plant food present, the less material should be added to a soil mixture.

Amounts of Fertilizer to Add to Soil Mixtures

Plant Food			Ounces per Bushel
ammonium nitrate	33%	N	¾
urea formaldehyde	38%	N	2
IBDU	38%	N	2
urea	45%	N	½
bone meal	13%	N	1
fish meal	11%	N	1
phosphorus	20%	P	2
phosphorus	40%	P	1
potash (potassium)	60%	K	½

Salt Stress

African violets are listed among plants which are the most sensitive to salt accumulation in their soil. Their delicate roots are easily killed when fertilizer salts become too concentrated. This condition is most likely to occur when you always water the African violets from the bottom.

It is possible for the salts, primarily sodium, to cause problems. Sodium is present if you have a water conditioner to remove the minerals from your drinking water. Table salt also contains sodium, if you need a handy reference as to how much sodium contributes to a salty substance.

Symptoms of salt stress from over fertilization of African violets are very similar in appearance to other plant problems caused by too little light, disease, and insects. Generally a plant's growth will suddenly slow down and the lower, older leaves begin to drop off. The main roots of the plant will die from salt toxicity. When this happens, the entire plant begins to wilt. If you have well-drained soil and have kept it only moderately moist then the wilting stage is probably the best symptom, along with a white crust on the soil surface, for diagnosing your plant's problem.

To overcome fertilizer salt stress you need to leach a large quantity of water through the soil mixture. This will flush out excess salts from the soil and give the African violets another lease on life. Should you be too late to save the plant, and it is one of your favorites, take several leaf cuttings and start some new plants.

After getting your leaf cuttings, one last attempt can be made to salvage the sick plant. Remove the plant from the pot and wash all the soil away from the roots. Repot the plant in a fresh soil mixture. Maybe the plant will survive this rough treatment, and maybe not. It is worth a try.

6

Potting Mixtures for African Violets

There are about as many different soil mixtures as there are African violet enthusiasts. Each grower has a very special mixture in which his or her plants thrive beautifully. The same mixture may or may not work for any other African violet grower. To come up with a single mixture agreeable to all would be impossible. This is why in this chapter several different types of soil mixtures are discussed, along with a list of the various ingredients from which you may choose.

After you have been growing African violets for a time, you will undoubtedly come up with your own special mixture, one that works best for the plants in your home and is adapted to your particular plant-care techniques.

The problems besetting most African violets in the home can very often be narrowed down to the type of soil mixture in which they are growing. You have your house and furnishings as comfortable as possible, making everything fit your particular life style. Why not do the same for your African violets. Their home is the potted soil in which their roots are growing. If you want a healthy, happy, vigorous flowering plant, give it a comfortable home. A well-prepared soil mixture is important to being successful with African violets.

Soil Mixture Ingredients

There seems to be no end to the possibilities when discussing the different kinds of materials available for special soil mixtures. Let your imagination go; and from past experience, I am sure you can quickly add to the list I have compiled.

Ingredients for Use in African Violet Soil Mixtures

woods earth	leaf mold	sand
peat moss (German,	vermiculite	bone meal
Canadian and Michigan)	rotted wood	garden loam
charcoal	calcine clay	sponge rubber
perlite,	sawdust	fish meal
cottonseed meal	compost	shredded fir bark
peat humus	seed hulls	crushed corncobs

One main goal, when mixing these materials together, is to develop a soil mixture with excellent drainage. Good drainage is required to protect African violets when you accidentally overwater them. The excess water will drain out the bottom of the pot and maintain a delicate balance between water and air in the soil in which roots are actively growing.

The key ingredient for every African violet mixture is humus or organic matter. Peat moss and pure humus are two excellent organic materials to use in soil mixtures. Both retain moisture well and allow excess water to drain through the pot. Organic materials also add a natural richness to the soil mixture and encourage African violets to do superbly.

Sphagnum peat moss is especially well suited for use in African violet soil mixtures. It has several characteristics that make it a good choice: 1) it is easy to find at almost any garden center; 2) it does not break down or decompose readily; 3) usually very little soil is present with it; 4) sterilization to rid the peat of unwanted pests does not ruin it, and 5) it can be purchased in several different grades (sizes).

Two ingredients, sand and garden loam, mentioned in the list of possible ingredients for African violet soil mixtures, need to be singled out for special comments. The use of very fine sand in a soil mixture should be discouraged; it adds very little to the mixture except weight. It can actually do more harm than good if you decide to use it and do not mix in the correct amounts. If you are determined to use sand, at least select sand which is coarse in size. Very fine sand (like that found on beaches) packs very tightly and causes the soil mixture to become too hard for good root growth. This is especially true when clayey soil is present in the soil mixture. A pure, washed sand is okay for starting cuttings.

Garden loam is a common term used for rich, organic soils. The actual composition of the loam will vary considerably. Very often it has a high percentage of clay and silt particles in it and therefore could be unsuitable for African violets. If using garden loam, select it carefully to get one as free of clay and silt as possible. One of the best sources of rich garden loam is the compost pile in your yard. The mixture of various types of organic materials and thin layers of soil forms a rich blend most plants love.

Before using compost material in potting mixtures it is a good idea to determine what was tossed on the compost pile before you try to grow African violets in it. It is very possible that some toxic materials may be present which would be harmful to your plants. A weed killer is often the culprit that lurks in the compost pile.

Acid Soil Mixtures Preferred

What is meant by an acid mixture? An alkaline one? How is something called pH related to African violets? These are questions every grower asks whenever the topic is mentioned. It is important to know a little about the topic, but you needn't become an expert on the subject.

The designation pH is used to tell you how acid or alkaline a soil mixture is. Small test kits are available at most garden centers for determining the pH number of a soil. By following the directions that come with the kit you will be able to check all your soil mixtures for proper pH reading.

Compare your number readings to the pH scale on the next page to determine whether your soil mixture is in the ideal range for African violets.

African violets prefer a soil mixture to be a little on the acid side. A pH of 6.8 to 6.9 would be perfect, but plants will also do quite well in a range of 6.4 to 7.4. When the pH is higher or lower than this, it is difficult for the roots to take the plant food from the soil mixture. Improper pH will also stunt the growth of the roots.

The ingredients you select for your soil mixture influence the pH of the mix. As previously mentioned, peat moss and humus are two excellent ingredients to use in a potting mixture. Both of these materials help to keep the soil mixture on the acid side of the pH scale.

After you have checked the pH of your soil mixture and discovered that the pH is too acid, you can add lime to the soil mixture and bring the pH up to the ideal range. The best time to do this is when you are mixing ingredients to formulate your soil mixture. It is possible to add lime to a potted plant, but it is a little more risky.

Basically there are three kinds of lime from which you can choose: pure limestone, dolomitic limestone, and hydrated lime. Of the three, dolomitic limestone is the best, because as it changes the pH of the soil mixture it adds two important plant foods (calcium and magnesium) to the mixture. Hydrated lime is considered a ''hot'' material which can very easily burn plant roots and cause severe damage. You must exercise extreme caution with this product.

Hydrated lime dissolves readily in water, and once it is thoroughly mixed it can be poured on the soil of a potted plant. Dissolve one-half ounce of hydrated lime in five gallons of water. Since this material can easily harm plants, be careful to measure the exact amount. Don't use the wrong size measuring spoon. Stir the solution thoroughly before using it. Be careful not to spill or pour any of this solution on your African violets. If you do, wash the plant off immediately to prevent any damage to it.

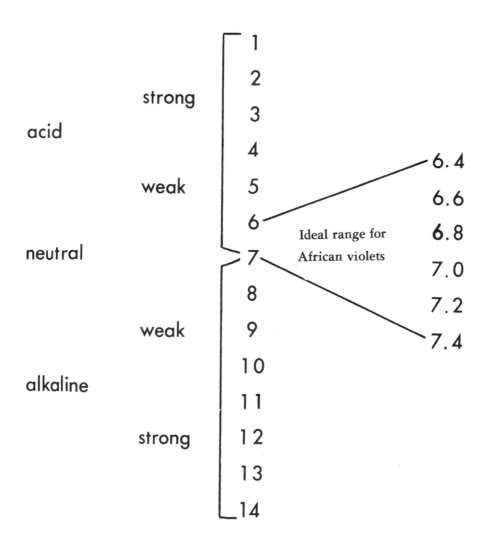

When buying dolomitic limestone, the size of the individual granules should be considered. The finer the material, the quicker it breaks down and goes to work on soil acidity. This means it will change the pH faster, but the lime will also dissolve and be gone from the soil mixture quicker. Usually a store will have just one type of limestone material, so you won't have a choice. But if you find both the coarse and the fine dolomitic limestone then use the fine material if the soil mixture is strongly acid, and the coarser if the pH is just below the ideal range of 6.4.

Purpose of the Soil Mixture

Often you are told to do this or do that when preparing the soil mixture, but you are never told why. Before looking into the various ways to use the ingredients we have discussed so far to create a soil mixture, let's take a little time out to find out the purpose of the mixture.

A soil mixture serves four basic functions which all African violets need for survival. The roots of the plant become anchored in the soil, allowing the plants to hold themselves up proudly to show off their flowery ornamentation. Plant food, so vital in all stages of the development of African violets, is stored in the soil mixture. Water, which is needed to allow a plant to absorb the plant food and carry on photosynthesis and other growth functions, is also stored in the mixture. Finally the last function of the soil mixture is to store the oxygen needed to keep plant roots alive.

Just about any kind of soil mixture you use will allow a plant to send roots down to anchor itself and store plant food. The trick is to create soil mixture that allows for proper balance between the water and air it needs to store for plant use. You want the soil to have equal proportions of air and water stored in the soil. This is one reason why the use of organic materials in the soil mixtures is stressed so much; it allows the excess water to drain through and keeps the air and water in proper balance.

Creating Your Own Special Mixture

African violets like a very porous, airy type soil mixture—one which is soft to the touch, fluffy and lightweight. The mixture will appear dark in color, with plenty of organic matter plainly visible. These are good characteristics to look for when buying or concocting a soil mixture for use in your home.

Endless variations of soil mixtures for African violets are possible. Each grower has a special mix, developed with tender loving care, mixed with a variety of ingredients, and the proportions of each used in the soil mixture labelled ''top secret.''

It doesn't matter so much what yours is, so long as your plants do well in it. I am absolutely positive that you'll get more enjoyment out of growing African violets in a special mixture which you discovered works well for you and your plants. With a little experimenting you can develop this special mixture.

When you first start out mixing your own ingredients, try to omit the soil. Your plants will do quite well in soilless mixtures. Eliminating the soil will greatly enchance your chances of being successful. After mastering the soilless mixtures, experiment by adding some soil to your mixes.

The problems you may encounter using soils in the mix should be known so you can avoid them. Soils vary a great deal in the amount of clay and silt present in them. Unless you are a soil scientist, it can be very difficult to estimate the percent of each in a soil.

It is the clay and silt that can ruin your potting mixture and cause your African violets to do poorly. When you mix soil and peat together, the coarser organic material will clog all the small air pockets. This forces the air out and allows water to be held in the mixture. When this happens, the plant roots die—and that's the end of your African violets.

Selecting the proper soil for use in the potting mixture and then mixing in the proper proportion of the other ingredients is important. Sandy soils are best. The sandier the better. The more sand a soil has in it, the less clay and silt it can contain.

Do your mixing by volume, just as you would if you were baking a cake. A measuring cup or a pint jar will work fine as a measuring tool. Never add more than 10 percent soil, by volume, to a potting mix. As little as 5 percent would even be better. A 10 percent soil mixture would be obtained by mixing one part soil to nine parts of whatever the other ingredients are. Remember this 10 percent rule when using a soil, and your mixtures should be successful.

A Look at Different Soil Mixtures

The same basic materials are used in most soil mixtures, only the proportions vary according to individuals. For African violets you want a soil mixture that remains loose and fluffy. This will guarantee adequate drainage and good air supply for healthy vigorous plants.

As stated before, you must experiment and create your own soil mixture, one that works well for your plants. To assist you in your experimenting I am going to list various types of mixtures for you to use as references. The combination of ingredients used here by no means covers all the different possibilities.

For African violets I prefer the mixtures without soil. Besides causing the problems already discussed, its use is a good way to introduce plant insects and diseases into your home. Soil sterilization will solve this problem, but it isn't always convenient.

Horticulturists at Purdue University have found that African violets will grow nicely in a mixture of equal parts of peat, vermiculite, and perlite. Other universities have in separate studies come to the same conclusion. Cornell University has come up with a mixture for African violets where one part sphagnum peat moss and one part vermiculite or perlite is used, narrowing down the ingredients to just two. You must keep in mind that these mixtures without soil will need to be fertilized a little more frequently.

A shredded peat mixed in equal parts with calcine clay forms another excellent potting soil for African violets. This mixture has worked well for one particular expert grower who has used it for years to produce prize-winning plants. The advantage of this mixture is its excellent drainage which always keeps the water and air in proper proportions in the mix. Good drainage also means there is less chance of salt accumulation in the soil mixture.

African violets prefer a slightly acid soil mixture and the peat-calcine clay combination gives it to the plants. Usually the pH will be near 6.8 to 7.0. Also, any mixture composed mostly of peat moss will have the slightly acid pH African violets need.

Using soil in the mixtures requires carefully measured proportions of all the ingredients to be used. Remember, keep the soil down to less than 10 percent of the total mixture.

1	part very sandy soil
6	parts sphagnum peat moss
3	parts vermiculite or perlite

1	part sandy loam soil
4	parts coarse washed sand
4	parts sphagnum peat moss
1	part lead mold

Although there is no guarantee that any given soil mixture will be perfect for all African violets, these two will give you an idea of the way to incorporate soil into your mixtures. Both of these mixtures were found to be excellent for the fibrous roots of African violets.

The use of garden loam as an ingredient was discussed earlier. Very often you will see it mentioned. Its actual use in the soil mixtures needs to be considered now. Garden loam has some silt and clay in it but by the time you mix it with the other ingredients the clay and silt particles will have been diluted to less than 5 or 10 percent of the total mixture.

Examples of Mixtures Using Garden Loam

Mixture #1	1	part garden loam
	4	parts calcine clay
	1	part coarse washed sand
Mixture #2	1	part garden loam
	5	parts leaf mold
	4	parts vermiculite or perlite
Mixture #3	1	part garden loam
	3	parts sphagnum peat moss
	3	parts shredded bark
	3	parts vermiculite or perlite

Crumbly Soil Mixture Best

Once you have mixed all the ingredients together it would be nice to know if it is a good mixture before you plant your favorite African violets in it. There is a quick test you can make that will tell you something about the mixture. Wet a cupful of the soil mixture until it is thoroughly damp. Let all the excess water drain out of the mixture, then place it in your hand and squeeze it very tightly together. When you open your hand the mixture should fall apart. It if doesn't, then use a knife and gently pick at it to see if it will crumble into a loose pile. Should the mixture remain a tight ball, it is not a good soil mixture for African violets.

Of course a better test for your specially mixed potting soil is how well your African violets do after they have been growing in it for a while. A beautiful plant with an abundance of flowers can tell a great deal about a mixture, and a dead African violet will tell a different story. If you see the plant is dying, remove it from the pot and place it in a fresh mixture of a different type.

There are several characteristics that denote a poor soil mixture. How the roots grow can tell you much. If the roots are massed all along the side of the pot and in the surface inch, the mixture is not a good one. A good soil mixture will have the roots growing throughout it. Often the main roots will grow down through the mixture, with its secondary branching roots growing right out to the pot's edges through the soil. Another characteristic of a poor mixture is poor drainage. Anytime a mixture stays wet for a long time it will eventually kill your African violets. Water forces out the air they must have to survive. When dry the same mixture becomes hard as a rock, making it impossible for roots to grow down through it.

If you have selected the proper ingredients and mixed them in correct proportions the mixture will be well drained, lightweight, and fluffy. You can always tell a good soil mixture by the overall appearance of the plants. An African violet cannot hide its feelings about the soil in which its roots are growing.

Prepackaged Soils

For convenience, you can buy African violet soil already prepackaged at most garden centers and larger department stores. This is an expensive way to obtain potting soil but if you need only a small amount, use it.

One major advantage of using prepackaged soils is that they are specially formulated to be very porous and open. This means good drainage and a better chance of growing healthy African violets. Occasionally some brands of packaged soil mixtures will not have any soil in them. African violets do well in soilless mixtures, but you will need to fertilize them more often. Lack of soil allows the plant food to be washed out the bottom of the pots. Often the label on the package will tell whether any soil is present.

Sterilization Gets Rid of Pests

Unless you are using prepackaged soil mixes, you need to kill any pests lurking in your soil mixture. Bacteria, fungi, and insects may be present by the billions, ready to strike down your African violets the instant they get the chance.

Heating the soil mixture or treating it with chemicals are the two choices for sterilizing your soil. Pick whichever one seems to fit your individual needs. Give careful consideration before deciding on chemical sterilization. Chemical additives do an excellent job of getting rid of the pests in the soil mixtures, but they are very toxic to humans. Because of the danger involved, I would avoid using them.

Most of the chemical soil sterilants are not made for home use but are meant for commercial plant growers to use in their larger operations. If you are determined to use a chemical soil sterilant, check your local nurseries and greenhouses to see if they have any for sale. Be extremely careful when using these materials.

PASTEURIZATION OF POTTING SOIL

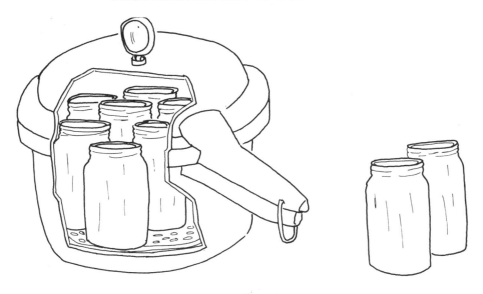

Use a pressure cooker to rid your potting soil of unwanted pests. Heat the soil-filled jars at fifteen pounds pressure for one hour.

Heat treatment of soil—or maybe a better term would be pasteurization of soil—is a safe and simple procedure you can use in the home. You will need to wet the soil mixture and let it stand for twenty-four hours prior to pasteurizing it. Generally there are two ways you can go about this pasteurization process.

Steam pasteurization seems to do the best job. This is the technique most frequently used by professionals at greenhouses and nurseries. The temperature of the soil is gradually raised to 180 degrees F., and then held there for thirty to forty-five minutes.

Use your pressure cooker at home to pasteurize your soil mixtures. The one you use for canning or bottling vegetables and fruits from your garden will work splendidly. Cover the bottom of the cooker with one-half inch to three-quarters of an inch of water. The rack supporting the jars should be above the level of the water. Whatever the capacity of the cooker, put the soil mixture into quart jars and fill it up. You could put fourteen to sixteen quarts in a sixteen-quart pressure cooker and have enough soil sterilized for potting twenty-five to thirty African violets. Heat the pressure cooker until the pressure inside reaches fifteen pounds. Hold it there for sixty minutes while the steam and heat pasteurize the soil mixture and free it of all pests.

Dry heat is the second pasteurization method you can use. Simply place the soil mixture in an oven, set the heat at 180 degrees F., and come back in one hour to remove the mixture from the oven. This method, however, has one drawback the pressure-cooker approach doesn't have. Sometimes the heat may bring out some rather unpleasant odors, so be sure you have a well-ventilated kitchen before you begin.

Do not let the temperature go above or below the 180-degree F. mark. Too high a temperature will cause some of the ingredients in the soil mixture to break down and the mixture will lose some of its value as a plant mix. If you let the temperature drop below 180 during the sterilization process, all the pests, especially the nematodes, will not be killed.

Put Plant Food in Your Soil

The easiest time to insure that your African violets have a good food supply is now. You have finished mixing the ingredients and sterilized the mixture. Now you are ready to mix the plant food into the mixture. There are several granular fertilizers available from which you may choose. Pick one that contains nitrogen, phosphorous, and potassium in equal amounts; these three plant foods are the most important to your African violets.

Novice gardeners often make a serious mistake when adding fertilizers to their soil mixtures. Incorporating fertilizer requires using very careful measurement. Don't over do it. By adding too much plant food you elevate the salt (from the plant food) content, a sure way to burn the African violet's delicate roots and possibly killing the entire plant. Don't make this novice's mistake.

Actual amounts of fertilizer to mix into a soil mixture are explained in Chapter 5 which deals with plant food and the requirements of African violets. You will be dealing with ounces of fertilizer material per bushel of soil mixture. This may not sound like much plant food, but it doesn't take much to do the job.

7

Pots, Potting, and Repotting

*P*ots and containers for growing African violets come in all sizes, shapes and colors. Only your imagination can limit you. Many containers are very attractive and excellent for decorating your home, but you must be certain that those you select are also suitable for African violets.

I have seen everything from tin cans, various kitchen utensils, wooden boxes, old teapots, glass jars, and worn-out coffeepots used for plant containers. Some of the containers will allow African violets to develop perfectly; in others the plants just can't adapt and do poorly. It is hard to find a container that beats the old-fashioned porous clay pot.

One point to consider when selecting an unusual pot or container is the ease with which the plant can be removed when it is time to transfer it into a bigger container. Often it will be necessary to cut and pry plants out of those odd-shaped containers. This rough treatment will mar their appearance and set their growth and development back several weeks.

Which Container Is Best

There are all kinds of pots and containers available, but some are more suitable than others for growing African violets. The best containers will always have a drain hole in the bottom. This insures an essential air supply to the root zone by allowing surplus water to drain away. Without a drain hole the water will accumulate in the pot, keep the soil mixture wet, and cause plant roots to die.

If you select a container without a drain hole, add a one-inch layer of charcoal in the bottom before adding the soil mixture. This will absorb any excess water that reaches the bottom of the pot. As the soil mixture dries out, this absorbed water will reenter the soil for the roots to use. Broken pieces of pots or small gravel on the bottom of the pot will also act as a good drainage reservoir.

Add a one-inch layer of charcoal to the bottom of any pot that does not have a drain hole. The charcoal readily absorbs water, helping to prevent a soggy soil from occurring. This moisture is released back into the soil as the plant needs it.

Either of these methods will work to prevent root damage in containers without drainage holes. The added material in the bottom of the containers allows for a little error in your watering judgment, provided you don't over-water every day.

Double potting African violets was explained in Chapter 3. This technique is an excellent one to use when you want to have a decorative planter located in a strategic location in your home. It allows you to combine the advantages of two different types of containers and minimizes the disadvantages of each.

Let's examine several different types of containers to find the characteristics of each. This will allow you to choose containers that best fit your particular circumstances.

Clay Pots

Red-clay pots are still the best containers available for growing African violets. They come in a wide range of sizes, have a drainage hole, and have matching saucers on which to set the pots. These pots are porous, which means that air can move through the pot and into the soil mixture. By the same token, soil moisture can move out through the pot and evaporate. When this happens, the soil dries out a little faster than in other types of containers.

Some gardeners claim that the porosity of clay pots is a disadvantage. But I don't agree. Air movement through the pot into the soil is essential for good root growth and healthy African violets. Also the slight loss of moisture helps to prevent the soil from becoming soggy and harmful to the African violets. As this moisture evaporates into the air it performs another important job for you—it helps to raise the relative humidity around the plant.

If you are on a routine watering schedule and paying attention to your plants, the advantages of using clay pots far outweigh any possible disadvantages.

Plastic Pots and Containers

It has become a common practice among African violet hobbyists to use plastic containers for growing their plants. If the plastic pots have a drain hole it will help to overcome the one major disadvantage of using these containers. Plastic will now allow moisture or air to move through the pot sides.

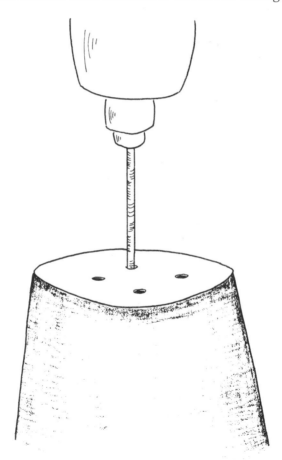

Glazed pots often do not have drain holes. Drill drain holes in the bottom of these pots to insure the plants will have healthy roots.

This leads to a wet, soggy, soil mixture if you aren't careful when watering. Water the African violets a little less frequently when using plastic containers.

Using a very porous soil mixture will also help to avoid having soggy soil. This type of mixture will allow the water to drain through quickly and maintain a proper balance of air and water in the root zone.

Plastic pots offer three very impressive features: they are lightweight, and therefore very easy to handle; they are easy to clean; and they come in a wide range of sizes, shapes, and colors.

Glazed Pots

You may call these ''ceramic'' pots since they have a glazed finish and were baked in an oven to harden them. When it comes to decorative pots, this group is hard to beat. Strawberry pots are especially beautiful, and African violets can be displayed very nicely in containers of this type.

Frequently glazed pots have a drain hole. But if not, you may use an electric drill and drill a hole in the bottom of the pot. Buy a special drill bit for this job and you won't have any problems. Support the pot with a block of wood on the opposite side you are drilling. Don't rush the job! Take your time and drill slowly or you may crack or break the bottom of the pot. Follow the same watering techniques as with plastic containers.

Metal Containers

Often an old copper tray or aluminum pot makes an attractive container for African violets. These metal containers will work fine provided they hold enough soil for healthy root growth.

The cultural requirements for growing African violets in metal containers is the same as those you encounter with the glazed and plastic pots. Again, be watchful for overwetting of the soil. Let it dry out between waterings and allow air movement into the root area.

What Size Pot to Use

Selection of a pot for your African violets is probably more important than you realize. The main reason you grow these plants is because of the gorgeous blossoms they produce. Flowering of the plants is closely related to the size of the pot in which they are growing.

An African violet will not flower abundantly when placed in a pot until the roots have completely filled the soil in the pot. If too big a pot is used, it will take the roots a long time to become crowded in the pot. Meanwhile you will be anxiously waiting several weeks or months for the formation of flower buds. Also the soil will remain too moist for long periods of time, and this results in a sour soil. This condition will let an infection called crown rot attack the plants.

In selecting a pot keep in mind that it should be only slightly larger than the soil ball on the African violet plant. A three-quarters of an inch space between the soil ball and pot sides is sufficient. New soil can be filled into this space, and the roots will grow into it quickly and without affecting the flowering.

Leaves hanging over the edge of the pot are a desirable feature. You'll have a healthier plant and a more attractive one by picking a pot small enough to allow this. Be careful, however, to keep the leaves from touching the rim of the pot.

One other point to remember when selecting a pot is its overall depth. Some pots are tall and skinny and others are short and squatty. Use short pots rather than tall ones because African violets have a tendency to be shallow-rooted.

What is the correct pot size? Well, it will vary according to the age and size of the African violet plant. When discussing pot sizes you should understand that the sizes given are for their diameter at the rims.

Leave three-quarters of an inch between the soilball and the new pot for additional soil when repotting an African violet. The roots will quickly grow into the fresh soil, renewing the vigor of the plant. Broken pieces of a clay pot on the bottom of the pot will prevent the soil from washing out the drain hole.

New plants, from seed or cuttings, should be first placed in pots that are two to two-and-a-half inches in diameter. Plants should be moved to a larger pot when eight to twelve leaves have formed. Often blossoms will have already begun opening before you need to move the plant into a larger pot.

Choose a three to four-inch diameter pot in which to transfer your nicely shaped African violets. These pots should be big enough for the lifespan of the plants. Pots of this size hold the correct amount of soil and the roots have no trouble filling into the mixture prepared for them. Eventually the plants will become slightly potbound and make a real bloomer out of them. A mature plant, except for a miniature African violet, will easily have a six to twelve-inch leaf spread, with overlapping leaves, creating an attractive plant that will be the envy of your friends and neighbors.

Very seldom will you need to select a pot larger than one measuring four inches in diameter. A single-crown plant does best in a smaller pot. If you let African violets develop more than one crown, called multicrowned, they must be planted in a larger pot to accommodate the extra size.

Guidelines to Follow When Potting

African violets are very rewarding plants to grow when given proper care. This includes following correct potting procedures. To be successful, use the following guidelines to direct you in potting your plants.

Guildeline #1

Prepare the soil mixture to meet the special requirements of your African violets. Be careful when adding fertilizer to the soil mixture. New, actively growing rootlets of African violets are very sensitive to fertilizer salts.

Guideline #2

Select correct size pots or containers for your plants.

Guideline #3

Drainage of excess water from a pot or container must be considered prior to potting your plants. African violets do not like ''wet feet'' and provisions must be made to insure that the soil mixture drains well.

Guideline #4

Thoroughly wet the soil mixture immediately following the potting of your plants. This helps to overcome the shock of transplanting and sets them off on a good start.

Guideline #5

Never expose a newly potted African violet to strong sunlight. Place it in filtered light for a few weeks until it has completely recovered from being moved into a new pot.

Guideline #6

Whenever moving seedlings, cuttings, or transplanting your plants lift as much of the soil mixture as possible with the plant. The more of a soil ball there is, the bigger the root system the plant will have. This is important to the survival of newly moved plants.

Guideline #7

The depth you place an African violet in a pot has a profound effect on its performance. Keep the soil level in the pot one-quarter of an inch below the rim of the pot. At the same time the crown should be even or slightly above the level of the rim.

Both of these suggestions concern the watering of your plants. A lower soil level allows you to water easily without washing soil out of the pot and making a mess. Having the crown elevated prevents the water from wetting it and causing crown-rot disease.

Guideline #8

Letting the plant wilt a little just prior to potting will help prevent any mechanical or physical damage from occurring during its handling. A lower moisture content in the plant tissue and cells reduces the brittleness of the leaf petioles (stems), thus reducing the number of leaves broken off during potting. Should you follow this guideline, then it is essential also to follow Guideline #4.

Guideline #9

If you have selected the clay pots in which to grow your plants, then there are three important steps to follow in order to insure a happy home for the plants.

Step #1

Be sure to sterilize your clay pots before using them. Elimination of disease and insect pests from pots is essential for the health of the plants.

Step #2

Moisture will escape from the soil mixture through the sides of a dry clay pot. To avoid this problem, presoak the pots in a bucket of water prior to potting the plants. This slows up the loss of water from the soil mixture and prevents a rapid drying out of soil which will damage the delicate roots.

Step #3

Preventing salt damage to your plants is not a difficult job. Coat the rims of the pots with a thin layer of wax. The beauty of using wax is that it is a transparent barrier which doesn't ruin the appearance of the pot. Molding aluminum foil around the rim is another simple technique.

I have briefly touched on nine very important points to remember when potting African violets. For a more detailed discussion of each point refer to other sections of this book.

Cleaning Your Pots

Dirty pots not only detract from the appearance of African violets but may harbor unwanted guests. Insects and disease organisms lurk in the old soil which is still present in a previously used pot. Therefore a thorough cleaning is necessary.

Cleaning the pots is not difficult. Take a garden hose and flush out any loose soil or debris. Next, fill a bucket with lukewarm water and immerse the pots for fifteen or twenty minutes. Scrubbing the pots after removing them from the bucket will loosen any crusted soil or salts. If all the rinsing and scrubbing still leaves the pots looking a little scruffy, place them in an empty bucket and pour boiling water over them until they are completely immersed, add a quarter cup of household bleach to the water, and let everything stand for two to three hours. Then remove the pots and thoroughly rinse them off with tap water. The pots should be sparkling clean.

You still may have some hidden problems lurking in your freshly cleaned pots which you may or may not wish to worry about. Bacteria, fungi, virus, and nematodes all could have survived the initial cleaning and still be hiding in the cracks and crevices of the pots. Chances are good that if you go ahead and pot your plants in these pots they'll be healthy anyway. But at the same time there is a chance that one of the diseases or insect pests will emerge and make your African violets sick.

Sterilization or pasteurization of pots will solve this problem for you. Heat treatment will work fine for pots. Just place the clean pots in the kitchen oven and set the temperature at 180 degrees F. After sixty minutes remove the pots from the oven. This should kill any pests which would have attacked your African violets.

One final point to remember: be absolutely sure that all pots are clean and free of soil or any debris. An awful odor may occur when heating the pots if you fail to inspect them first.

Repotting Technique

Eventually you will have some African violets that outgrow their homes and must be repotted in larger pots. Most often this will occur when you have seedlings or young cuttings growing in the two to two-and-a-half-inch diameter pots. Occasionally a mature plant will become extremely potbound and a larger pot will be needed for this plant. Repotting is a relatively easy process and a very enjoyable pastime if you know what you are doing.

Determining when an African violet needs to be repotted is best accomplished by actually looking at the roots. Take a pencil and gently push it against the soil through the drain hole. The plant and its soil ball will usually

When a plant will not slip easily from the pot insert a pencil through the drain hole and gently push against the soilball. Easing a plant from the pot this way will not harm it in any way as long as you are careful.

come out with ease. If there are masses of roots exposed around the edge of the soil ball it is time to repot the plant.

Sometimes you will be unable to force the plant loose with a pencil. This is a good indication that roots are growing around the inside edge of the pot. When this happens it is a good bet that it is time to repot the plant. Another excellent indicator of a healthy root system is when roots can be seen growing out of the drain hole. You can be sure the plant needs repotting when you see this happening.

If you are using pots or containers without drain holes, you may be able to lightly tap the sides of the pots and cause the soil ball to slide out for inspection of the roots. Your other choices are to go by the overall appearance of the plant, or simply repot the plants on a regular six-month schedule.

Removing a plant from the pot only to discover it is not yet ready to be repotted will not harm it if you are careful. Shake a little of the old soil mixture off the roots and add some fresh soil to the pot. This will increase the vigor of the plant by giving the roots a new source of plant food. Now, slip the plant back into the pot.

Removal of a plant from a pot is not a difficult task. A few gentle taps against the side of the pot with the heel of your hand should cause the soilball to slide out. You must remember to support the soilball in the palm of your other hand as it separates from the pot.

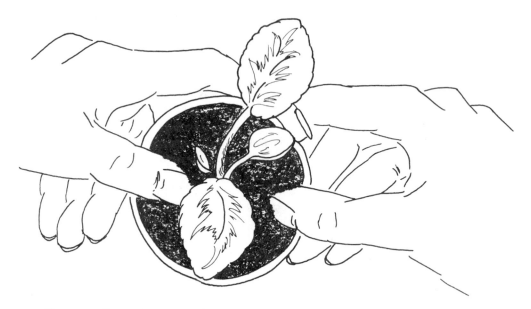

Use your fingertips to gently firm up the soil when potting.

Handle Your Plants Gently

Handling African violets should be done carefully whenever you remove them from a pot. These delicate plants are easily damaged if roughly treated. Take the pot in one hand and slip your other hand underneath the leaves. Your fingers should be forked on either side of the crown, with your palm touching the rim.

Tip the pot so the plant is tilted downward at a 45-degree angle. The rim of the pot will be resting on the palm of your hand. With your free hand gently tap the sides of the pot and rotate the pot slowly as you try to loosen the soil ball. The soil should break loose easily when this procedure is used and leave the plant in your hand ready to be placed in a new pot.

Occasionally the soil ball will be stubborn and stick to the sides of the pot. A wet soil will not slip out of the pot as easily as a dry soil. Do not try to pull the plant out or you will damage it. Try rapping the pot a little more firmly; if nothing happens, then another technique must be employed.

Run a long, thin knife along the inside of the pot. This will break the stubborn soil ball loose. Again, be careful not to damage the plant while doing this. Next, pick up the pot, tip it over, and again gently rap the sides with your hand. The plant and its soil ball should slip out freely.

Putting the plant into a new pot with fresh soil around it will make it more vigorous. The new soil should be pushed down with your fingers along the soil ball and pot sides. Never use a stick or knife handle. Your fingertips are very sensitive so you can easily tell if you are pushing too hard. You want the soil firmly packed in the pot.

8

Increasing Your Plants by Propagation

*E*veryone who has grown African violets knows the value of starting new plants from the old ones they have. In terms of money alone, the savings can add up to a tidy sum when you increase the number of your own plants at home. Going out and buying several new African violet plants can be expensive. The satisfaction you will get from working with African violets and producing your own new plants is truly one of the real joys of growing African violets.

Propagating your plants not only increases your own collection of African violets; you'll also have extra plants to use as gifts for special occasions or maybe just as a token of friendship and appreciation for someone close to you.

'How often have friends admired your African violets? Probably every time they entered your home and saw how lovely they are. "What a beautiful plant; where did you get it?" Or, "Boy, how come your African violets always look so nice?" These questions are compliments in disguise; they also convey the hidden meaning, "Gee, I wish I had one of those beautiful African violets!"

By having a few extra plants around the house you could very easily surprise the "secret admirers" by giving them one as they left for home. The fun of suprising your friends with a special living gift will make all of the work which has gone into propagating your plants well worthwhile. Your reputation as an African violet expert will spread with each new plant you give away.

Sexual or Vegetative Propagation

When you are considering starting new plants from old African violets

103

you have two methods of propagation from which to choose—sexual and vegetative. Sexual refers to growing new plants from seed; vegetative means using some part of old plants to form new ones.

Patience is required when working with seed. If you collect the seed from plants it requires you to do some pollinating. By pollinating I mean taking the pollen, found in the yellow parts (anthers) of the flower, and transferring it to the stigma (female part of the plant). Take a small piece of cardboard or heavy paper and place it under the yellow anthers. Gently tap the flower until the dustlike pollen is deposited on the paper. Touch the pollen to the female portion of another African violet blossom and the pollination process will be complete. In nature, bees do this job as they visit the various flowers in search of nectar. Within hours, fertilization will have occurred. Five to six months later the seed will be ready to harvest. You may find it simplier and more convenient to buy packets of seeds.

Those who grow African violets as serious hobbyists should be pollinating their own plants and starting new plants from seed. The purpose of using seed is to aid in the quest for new and better plants. Imagine the thrill of discovering a new variety and being able to name it. You'll have the satisfaction of knowing you are one of the select few who have introduced a new plant for the entire world to enjoy.

Vegetative propagation is the simplest technique for increasing your collection. It is as simple as snipping off a leaf or dividing an overgrown plant into several smaller ones. The big advantage of vegetatively reproducing plants is that all the new ones will look exactly like their parents. With the seed you produce many plants which are entirely different than their parents due to gene recombinations that occurred when the seed was formed.

Two basic techniques are used in vegetative propagation—crown division and cuttings. The most popular method is taking a leaf (cutting) and rooting it in water or soil mixtures. The ease of taking a cutting from an African violet is one of the main reasons for this plant's popularity. Also, if a friend wants a start from your favorite plant the removal of a single leaf will not be noticeable.

The purpose of taking a cutting or splitting a crown is to produce another plant identical to the parent plant. By doing this the new plant may be referred to as a ''clone,'' a term which simply means that the plants were propagated vegetatively and are identical to parent plants.

Leaf Cuttings

One of the most fascinating occurrences in nature is the ability of a plant to produce an entirely new plant from a leaf cutting. This is no easy task. Highly specialized plant cells and chemical compounds are involved. Propagation of plants from leaf cuttings has been used for several hundred years by plant lovers.

The most popular method of vegetatively starting a new plant from an

African violet is to remove a leaf and root it. You may hear the terms "cuttings" and "slips" used when referring to leaf removal. A "cutting" would be more appropriate, because a leaf and part of its petiole are all that is removed. I have always thought of a "slip" as taking off a stem of a plant which has several leaves attached to it. Either term is acceptable in garden circles, but I'll stick with "cutting" when discussing the various aspects of propagating African violets.

Regardless of terminology, the selection of the best leaves to use as cuttings is important if you are to be successful. The leaf should not be an old one or an immature one. Pick one that is very healthy, a vigorous grower, and of a nice dark-green color. Usually the leaf will be removed from the inner circle of the rosette of leaves. If you are working with a variegated African violet the cutting must have some green color (chlorophyll pigment) present. All-white leaves will not produce new plants; instead they shrivel up and die since they cannot manufacture any food for themselves.

Be sure to label each cutting you take from your plants so they can be identified later. It is fun to keep track of your African violets and watch your collection grow. When you give new plants to friends it is nice to be able to tell them exactly from which plant it was originally selected. You'll also be able to tell them the name of the particular variety, a little of the history of the plant's development in your home, and the color of the blossoms.

Use a sharp knife, a razor blade or scissors to cut the leaf away from the parent plant. Leave one-and-a-half inches of leafstalk attached to the leaf in your initial cut; you may wish to trim the stalk shorter, once it is in front of you on a table and is more accessible. If you are working with miniature African violets it will be difficult to find a leaf with one-and-a-half inches of leafstalk. In this case leave the stalk as long as possible for the best results.

Making the Final Cut

Trimming the end off the leakstalk just prior to placing a cutting in water or rooting mixture is more important than you probably realize. The number of new plantlets formed from a cutting depends on the way you trim the leafstalk. You want to expose as much of the leafstalk surface as possible at the cut end. If you make a blunt, square cut there is less exposed stalk at the cut than if you make the cut at an angle (Figure 1). To increase the exposed leafstalk surface even more, cut it off in a V shape (Figure 2). Another technique is to split the end of the leafstalk (Figure 3). You'll obtain more new plantlets per cutting if you follow the examples shown in Figures 2 and 3.

New roots develop from a layer of specialized cells (parenchyma) found in the leafstalk. These cells exist throughout the stalk, but those closest to the vascular bundles (plumbing through which the food and water move in the plant) seem to play a major role in the formation of roots. The buds which will eventually develop into new little plantlets arise from the surface (epidermis) of the leafstalk.

105

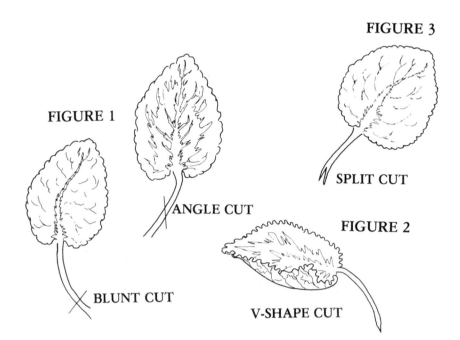

FIGURE 3

SPLIT CUT

FIGURE 1

ANGLE CUT

FIGURE 2

BLUNT CUT

V-SHAPE CUT

It should be mentioned here that it is possible to root a leaf without a leafstalk being present. Very often when you do it this way the leaf will produce a sport or a new plant which is not identical to the parent plant. Such plants are often inferior and do not have many of the desirable features you have learned to enjoy with other African violets. For this reason it is always a good idea to have some leafstalk attached to the cuttings.

Control Mites Now

Insect pests are a perpetual threat to African violets, especially mites. These little bugs are always difficult to kill. One of the easiest times to rid a plant of them is when you are taking cuttings. Once you have the leaf and leafstalk separated from the parent plant, dip it in a miticide (mite killer) such as aramite. Completely immerse the leaf so it is wetted all over. After removal from the solution, let the leaf surfaces dry off for twelve to eighteen hours before rinsing with warm water. During this waiting period keep the leafstalk in water as if it were being rooted. This dipping procedure will rid your new cuttings and future African violets of mites for quite a while.

Starting Cuttings in Water

Leaf cuttings may be rooted in either water or a special rooting mixture. Both ways will work very satisfactorily provided you follow the correct procedures. Here the rooting in pure water will be discussed, followed by rooting in special mixtures. Consider each way and then select the one which best fits your particular needs. Consider also both ways for your first attempts at propagating African violets. The personal experience gained by actually trying the two techniques will help you to make the best choice.

Cuttings may be very easily started in water. Tap water will work fine, but rainwater or water from a dehumidifier is better. Both are free of salts and chlorine which inhibit root formation.

Containers used for rooting may be clear or tinted. I prefer a clear container so I can readily see when the roots are forming, how fast the new plantlets are growing, and the water level in the container.

These two leaves being rooted in water are being held in place by aluminum foil. Two holes were punched through the foil so that the leaves could be inserted into the water.

Usually starting cuttings in water is limited to when you have one or two cuttings you wish to work with. If you have ten to twenty cuttings then it is easier to root them in a special rooting mixture.

Now you're ready to put your trimmed leafstalk into the water. It is generally agreed by African violet growers that the leaf should not come in contact with the water or the sides of the container. (This is not a steadfast rule, however, for I have successfully rooted leaf cuttings which were half immersed in water and touching the container). To be safe, let only the leafstalk stick in the water.

Various methods have been devised to hold the leaf up out of the water. The simplest I have found is to mold a piece of aluminum foil over the top of the container and around the edges, then cut a small slit in the center of the foil for the leafstalk to be slipped through and into the water. You may place two or more leaf cutting in a single container filled with water provided that the leaves do not become so crowded they touch one another.

Place container with leaf cuttings in a bright, sunny window. Be sure that direct sunlight does not touch the cuttings; filtered light is best. If possible, pick a location with a constant 70 degrees F. and high humidity. All these conditions combined will encourage the fastest rooting of your cuttings.

You can expect new roots to begin developing in four to six weeks. If a cutting hasn't developed any roots by six weeks then chances are it never will. You have probably selected an older leaf which has lost the power to produce new plants. Next time select a younger, more vigoroulsy growing leaf from the center of a plant.

The water in the container may become stagnant if you have to wait four weeks or longer for roots to form. To avoid this, add fresh water as it evaporates or is used by the plant. Should a leaf rot while in the water and you have other cuttings in with it, move them to fresh water in another container. Once the water is contaminated by a rotten leaf, it will go to work on healthy cuttings and ruin them also.

Transfer the leaf cuttings into individual pots when the new plantlets are one to one-and-a-quarter inches tall. The soil mixture in the pots should be moist so the delicate rootlets won't die after all this time. Place these new plants in a bright spot in your home where they will receive plenty of filtered sunlight. Before long they will be filling out the pot and producing flowers for your enjoyment.

Start Your Cuttings in Rooting Mixtures

Rooting leaf cuttings in a soil mixture is ideal if you are working with several leaf cuttings. A single cutting placed in a small pot will also do well. In this case it just depends on whether you prefer to use pure water or a soil mixture. Both will do an excellent job.

While talking with friends about placing leaf cuttings in a soil mixture, I am sure you have heard of several different soil mixtures you should use.

108

Often African violet leaves are rooted in individual pots. When using this technique a little more attention must be given to keeping the soil mixture continually moist.

Each hobbyist seems to have a special mix that works perfectly and chances are that any of these mixes will also work for you.

All rooting mixtures must have the ability to absorb large quantities of water and at the same time allow the excess water to drain out of the container. Air in the soil mixture is as important to root development as is moisture. Some materials that work well to meet these essential requirements are: peat, vermiculite, very coarse sand, perlite, and crushed corncobs. Equal proportions of three or more of these materials will do a good job. You may elect to go to a garden center and buy regular African violet potting soil. If you do, add peat or vermiculite to the mix to make it more porous.

Common Rooting Mixture

2 parts vermiculite
2 parts peat moss
1 part prepackaged African violet soil mix

The use of a sterilized soil mixture is essential for rooting cuttings. The leaf and leafstalk are very vulnerable to disease attacks while trying to produce roots and new plants.

Rooting Mixture Containers

Now you are ready to select a rooting container. Just about anything will do: old fish aquariums, plastic kitchen containers, glass or metal cake pans, or even ice cube trays. Ideally a shallow container one or two inches deep, with drain holes, will be your best choice. An often overlooked container is the plastic flat your bedding plants come in every spring from local garden stores. These are a good depth and have drainage holes. If you use a deeper container without drain holes, add charcoal to the bottom of the container before filling it with a rooting mixture.

Ideal temperatures in the rooting mixture and around the plant are easily determined; however, it is difficult to achieve these temperatures all the time in your home. As a reference I will briefly touch on these temperature requirements and how you may obtain them.

The root zone temperatures should range from 70 to 75 degrees F. Several techniques may be employed to warm the mixture to this temperature range. The most sophisticated is the use of special electric heating cables specifically designed for this job. Prior to putting soil mixture in a container place the heat

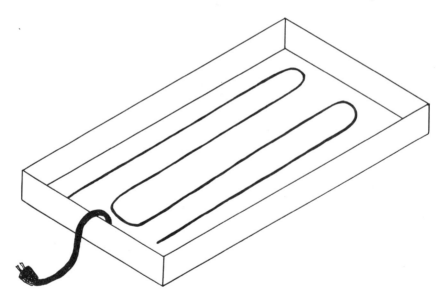

Commercially made soil warming boxes are available. The heating elements are attached to the bottom of the container. Once the soil mixture is poured into the container the heat is kept at the proper temperature for maximum rooting of the cuttings placed in the soil.

cable uniformly on the bottom of the container, then cover it with the mixture. The best way to think of this technique is to compare it with an electric blanket. You can control the heat in the soil mixture by turning the controls "on" or "off."

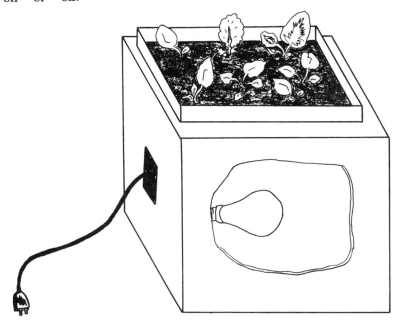

Place the container holding the cuttings on a specially built box with a light bulb inside. The bulb will release a sufficient amount of heat to keep the soil mixture warm, causing the cuttings to root more quickly.

Another way to heat the root zone is to build a box on which to set the rooting container. Inside the box, wire one incandescent light bulb. Use a low-wattage bulb to maintain a constant temperature in the soil mixture.

Air temperature around your cuttings should be 65 to 70 degrees F. Usually the air temperature is controlled by what you are personally comfortable with in your home. If you do not maintain the air and soil mixture at these ideal temperatures all the time do not worry about it. It just means that if may take a few extra days for the cuttings to develop roots and new plantlets.

Use of a Rooting Hormone

Before actually placing leaf cuttings in the rooting mixture there is a special rooting powder you can buy. This whitish gray powder is called a

111

growth-hormone. By placing a small portion of this powder on the leafstalk, root development may be quickened. This technique has been found successful by some researchers; others have stated that the hormone actually inhibits the development of new plantlets. For this reason I would suggest treating only a few cuttings if you want to try a rooting hormone and compare the results. These hormones are available at a reasonable price in most garden centers.

Application of the hormone is simple. Just push the leafstalk—after it is trimmed and ready to be placed in the soil mixture—into the powder one-eighth to one-quarter inch, gently shake the loose powder off and leave the leaf on a tabletop for fifteen to twenty minutes before placing it in the rooting mixture.

Placing Cutting in Rooting Mixture

To place a leaf cutting in the rooting mixture make a depression in the mixture with your finger. The depression should be approximately three-quarters to one inch deep. Place trimmed tip of the leafstalk in the depression and gently but firmly push the soil mixture against it. Always use your fingers for this job, not a pencil or a stick. Plant tissue is delicate and by using your fingertips you are more aware of the pressure you are exerting around the leafstalk.

Frequently the cuttings will lean over and touch the soil mixture. This should be avoided to prevent the leaves from becoming spotted. Use a toothpick or wooden matches (heads cut off) as props to hold the cuttings up from the surface of the mixture.

Cuttings placed in the soil mixture may take longer to develop new roots

Often a leaf cutting will rot when it comes into contact with the pot. To prevent this from occurring prop the leaf up with toothpicks.

112

than those placed in pure water. However, there is less chance of the newly rooted plants dying when transferring them from the rooting mixture to a pot.

Once the cuttings are placed in the rooting mixture it is essential that the mixture is kept moist at all times. It should feel damp to your fingers. If you can see water glistening in the light then you are keeping it too wet. Soggy mixtures cause the leafstalk to rot.

Miniature Greenhouse for Cuttings

When cuttings are placed in the rooting mixture they need a constant source of moisture. It is simple to keep the rooting mixture moist, but it is also easy to forget about it. Newly formed roots will shrivel up and die if you let the soil mixture dry out. This is something you do not wish to happen and can easily be avoided.

Creating a miniature greenhouse for African violet cuttings to root in is the answer. By covering the cuttings you confine the immediate area around them to a small microenvironment conducive to rapid plant development. The humidity will be very high, and the temperature just right for rooting to occur.

For rapid rooting and plantlet formation place your cuttings in a miniature greenhouse. Clear plastic draped over four sticks is an easy way to construct your own special propagation unit.

You will not have to worry about watering the cuttings in your small greenhouse. The cover will trap moisture and keep the rooting mixture moist for a long time. At the same time the humidity is so high that often it condenses on the sides of your little greenhouse. When this happens, remove the cover and wipe off the excess moisture. Wait two to three hours before replacing the cover. This gives the cuttings a brief break and allows them to dry off for a short time.

113

The cover you select for your miniature greenhouse can be just about anything. Glass or plastic cake-pan covers work very well. Aquariums covered with glass make excellent miniature greenhouses. Some people simply take a plastic bag, set the cuttings inside, and tie the bag at the top. This will work, but is not as attractive as some of the other methods.

Taking Care of the Cuttings

Remember that a leaf cutting is alive and expends a lot of energy to stay alive and produce a new African violet for you. Give it nourishment every fourteen days to replenish its energy and allow for rapid plant development. Go ahead and use the fertilizer solution you already have mixed for your African violets, but dilute it again with a cup of fresh water to each cup of fertilizer solution. This reduces the concentration of the fertilizer nutrients and prevents the salts from damaging tender young rootlets.

Should a cutting start to die before the plantlets are big enough to be transferred to a pot, you must take some preventive action or you may lose the new plants also. As soon as it is obvious that a cutting is dying, remove it by cutting off the leafstalk just above the new plantlets. Try not to disturb the roots or plantlets any more than is necessary while cutting off the dead leaf. Hopefully the new growth is mature enough to make it on its own and will be able to continue and become a beautiful African violet.

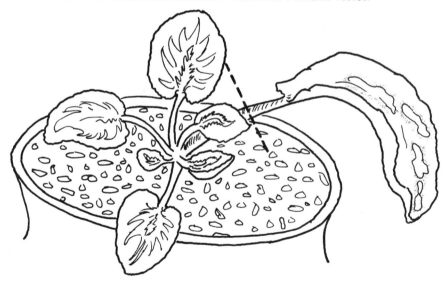

Removal of the parent leaf or cutting is necessary when it becomes sick. This will reduce the chances of the newly formed leaves from becoming sick and dying.

Do not expose the cuttings to any direct sunlight; only filtered light is necessary for root and plant development. Artificial lighting works well for rooting of cuttings. Place the fluorescent lights four to five inches above the cuttings for the best results. As the plants grow upward adjust the lights up also.

You can expect to see your first roots developing in about four to six weeks. New shoots or plantlets will begin appearing in ten to sixteen weeks. From cutting to first bloom the time will vary according to the variety of the African violet. A five to eight-month waiting period should produce the first blossoms. When this day arrives, you have achieved your goal of producing another beautiful African violet for your enjoyment or to give as a gift.

Potting New Plants

After the new plantlets have reached one to one-and-one-quarter inches in height you can begin transferring them into individual pots or containers. Use a fork or spoon to gently lift out the new plants from the rooting mix-

Whenever removing the young plantlets from the rooting mixture for potting, care must be used to avoid damaging the roots. Gently lift plantlets out, allowing as much soil as possible to cling to the roots.

ture. Several plants often develop from each leafstalk. If you want a hugh African violet plant, go ahead and pot all the plants in one pot. You'll end up with a multicrowned African violet. Single-crowned plants can be obtained by very carefully cutting apart the individual plants and potting each by itself.

Use your fingertips to gently pack the soil mixture around the newly potted plants. This will anchor the plants firmly into the pot until the roots can spread out into the new soil mixture. Top watering with warm water is most beneficial to the newly transplanted African violets.

Division of Crowns

Often African violets will grow to a size you do not wish to transfer to a larger pot. Or maybe you don't like the appearance of a large plant which is too dominating for your decorating scheme. In either case, these plants have literally grown themselves out of a spot in your home unless you do something with them. One very simple solution to this problem is to split the crown of the large plant into several individual plants.

Splitting the crown of any African violet must be done by one of two methods: division or separation, depending on whether you are dealing with one or more plants. Some confusion always surrounds these two gardening terms. Before discussing the particular steps involved with each technique, let's define the terms so you understand how they differ. Division deals with dividing a single plant which is multicrowned but has only one root system. When there are several individual crowns, each with its own individual root system, then separation is the technique you would use.

Now let's look at a few details on crown division and how to do it successfully. First, let the soil dry out before starting; this will make the job easier. Gently tap the plant loose from its container and place it on a newspaper or workbench. With your fingers work as much of the dry soil mixture away from the roots as possible. After completing this phase of the operation you should be able to readily see all the crowns of the plant and their root system.

With a sharp knife or scissors carefully cut through the crowns until each one is divided from the others. Try to retain as big a root system with each crown as you possibly can. Take the new crowns and immediately plant them in pots. The soil mixture should be premoistened and kept moist for a few days after the division of the crowns. After that, let the soil mixture remain on the dry side for two to three weeks to force new root growth and allow the plants to get over the shock of transplanting.

Separation of a multicrowned African violet is not as difficult a job as the division process. Again, with separation, you need to let the soil mixture dry so the plant can be more easily removed from the pot. Also the soil will cling

116

DIVISION

Use a sharp knife to cut apart crowns of the plant, which share a common root mass. Allow as much of the root system to remain attached to the individual plants as possible. Often one of the crowns will not have enough roots to keep the plant alive. When this happens it becomes necessary to place it in a special rooting mixture until it is ready to be placed in a separate pot. The last step is to give the plants ample water.

SEPARATION

Allow the soil to dry so that the individual plants and their root masses can be gently pulled apart. Pot and water each plant immediately for the best chances of a successful operation on your multicrowned African violets.

better to the roots, making it less likely for you to damage the delicate roots.

Once the plant has been removed from the pot and is out where you can easily examine it, determine how best to perform the operation. A multicrowned plant will have thick clumps of leaves rising from each crown. Very carefully pull the crowns apart and try not to knock off anymore soil from the roots than is absolutely necessary.

The real trick to successfully separating the crowns is to maintain as much of the soil mixture as possible with the roots of each crown. This will make it easier for the new plant to get a rapid start in its new pot. For the first month, after the initial watering of the new plant, be careful not to overwater. Your first instinct may be to water often, but the plant really needs only a moderate supply of water to keep it happy.

One other source frequently overlooked by African violet growers for obtaining additional plants is the ''suckers'' found growing on a mature plant. By definition, a sucker is a new plant which has developed from the base of an established plant.

Suckers can be cut off from the parent plant whenever they are big enough for you to handle easily. Use a sharp knife to make the cut, then immediately place the suckers in water or a soil mixture so they will root. Within a few weeks new roots will have developed and you can transfer the plants to pots.

Rejuvenating Necky Plants

When an African violet has reached maturity its older leaves will begin to drop off and expose the underneath parts of the plant. This is a very natural aging process that affects the appearance of the plants.

You should not toss the plant away even when the main stalk is bare for three or more inches above the soil surface, a condition African violet hobbyists call "necky." It is very simple to rejuvenate a plant with this problem by cutting off the stalk at the soil surface, and placing the top of the plant in fresh water until new roots form.

NECKY PLANT

As a plant grows older the lower leaves will eventually die and need to be removed. When enough leaves are gone to expose the main trunk of an African violet the term *necky* is used to described the plant.

Follow the steps listed here, and your "necky" plants will be as good as new in three or four weeks.

Step #1   Cut off the main stalk of the plant at the soil surface.

Step #2   Trim the stalk so that only two to two-and-one half inches remains below the rest of the plant.

Step #3   Scrape the stalk with a knife or spoonhandle to roughen up the plant's cell tissue. This encourages root formation.

Step #4   Lay the plant aside, and allow the stalk to air dry for thirty minutes.

Step #5   Place the stalk in water, vermiculite, or perlite until new roots form.

Step #6   Transfer to rooted plant to a pot. Wait two weeks, then begin feeding the plant a high phosphorous and potassium plant food. This will encourage the plant to start flowering again.

Two big advantages to using this technique on your aging African violets are: 1) the plants will begin flowering again very soon after being repotted, 2) restoring the vigor to an old plant means you'll be able to enjoy its beauty for many more years.

African Violets from Seed

The miracle of a seed germinating and developing into a lovely plant is fascinating. Watching your plants grow from seed gives you the awesome feeling that you are creating something new. And indeed you are!

When growing an African violet from seed the chances of the new plant being identical to any other one is very remote. The genetic code built into each seed will be different than that of another seed. Sometimes the changes will be so slight you may not even notice them; at other times the differences will be astounding.

It will take longer for you to obtain a mature, flowering African violet when you start with seed. The actual length of time will vary according to the variety of the African violet. Usually you will see the first blossom in about one year's time. Some plant varieties can be stubborn and take longer to produce flowers.

A proper germination bed must be prepared prior to seeding. Much of your success with developing African violets from seed will depend on your choice of soil mixtures. A clayey, poorly drained soil mixture will almost always cause problems for the young seedlings as they are trying to grow.

If the germination bed is kept continually wet, two diseases (pythium and gray mold) will attack the plants. The end result is the loss of your seedlings. Sterilization of soil mixture is a must if you are to avoid disease problems from overwatering.

Moisture must be retained by the soil mixture to insure seed germination and plant development. Good drainage can be assured by proper selection of a rooting mixture. Peat moss makes a good ingredient in the mixture

120

because of its ability to absorb moisture and at the same time let the excess water drain on through. You may add vermiculite or perlite to the peat moss. The mixture on which the seeds are to be sown should be similar to that which you will use later for potting new plants.

Select a container deep enough to hold at least two inches of soil mixture. Drainholes in the bottom of this container are essential. The plastic plant holders (flats) you get when buying spring bedding plants are ideal as containers. Pack the soil mixture loosely into a container.

Seeds from an African violet are so small they are dustlike in fineness. Carefully sprinkle the seeds as uniformily as possible on the surface of the premoistened soil mixture. Do not try to cover the seeds with any soil mixture; just leave them undisturbed on the surface of the mixture. After seeding, cover the container with a plate of glass (an old windowpane will work). Leave some space between the container and the glass for air circulation. The cover helps to keep seeds moist and the humidity high.

Seeds you have collected should be dried for a short period prior to being used. At least two to four weeks of air drying should be sufficient. Some African violet growers have been successful planting the seeds immediately after removing them from the plant. Chances are they have left the seedpots on the plant long enough for the seeds to have already dried and reached maturity before harvesting.

After you have the seeds sown and the glass cover securely in place, set the container in a warm sunny spot. Direct sunlight should not fall on the seeds. Air temperature around the seeds should be 65 to 75 degrees F. Temperatures slightly lower than this will allow the seeds to germinate but it will take them longer. When seeds are kept at the ideal temperatures you should see small roots and plants sprouting in three to four weeks. Some seeds may require longer to germinate, so don't give up if only a few plants come up in the first month. Often the longer-germinating seeds will develop into African violets with superior flowers and nicer foliage. After two or three months toss out any material which hasn't produced new plants.

Watering the seeds until they germinate is an easy task. You merely need to mist them frequently enough to keep them moist. This shouldn't have to be done more than one or two times. This gentle spray will be sufficient to cause the seeds to swell and begin the journey to becoming majestic African violets. The reason for using a fine mist spray of water is to avoid disturbing the seeds. Do not use any fertilizer solution for misting the seeds. Fertilizer should not be added to the watering schedule until the seedlings have developed two to four leaves, then fertilize with a diluted solution once every two weeks.

Trying to sow small African violet seeds uniformly over the soil mixture is a difficult task. I'm sure many of the seeds ended up bunched together, and when they germinated some of the plants were too close together. When this happens, it is a good idea to move them apart from one another within the same container until they mature enough to be moved into individual pots.

The time to begin this intermediate planting is when seedlings are in the four-leaf stage of development or about one-half inch tall. Carefully remove

121

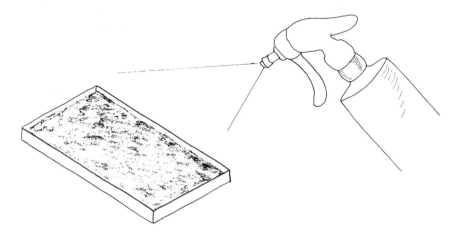

The best way to water the tiny seeds planted in this container is to spray the water on as a fine mist.

the plants and replace them in the container at least one inch apart. Handle these young seedlings very carefully as they are very tender and easily damaged.

African violet seedlings should be moved into individual pots when they have grown enough for the leaves of the different plants to touch. At this time the plants will be approximately two inches in diameter. New plants from seed will be ready for potting in six to eight weeks. At that time place them with your other African violets and schedule their care along with all your other plants.

When you transplant African violet seedlings try to take as much of the soil with the plant as possible; the tender rootlets will survive the move much better if you do. A fork or knife works well in lifting the plants from the mixture. Gently pry the seedlings up. So long as you take your time and treat the seedlings with tender loving care, chances are excellent that all your seedlings will survive the ordeal.

9
African Violet Pests and Other Problems

Whether you have a beautiful African violet collection or just a single plant in your home, why risk the chance of ruining their appearance. After all, if you didn't enjoy the natural beauty of African violets you wouldn't even bother having them in your house. Unnecessary exposure of the plants to disease, insects, and physiological stresses is senseless and should be avoided.

Physiological stress deals with the improper care of African violets. Paying proper attention to your plants will prevent problems of this type from ever occurring. The common sources of disease and insect problems is the introduction of a new African violet into the home and using a soil mixture which hasn't been sterilized. Although you should always be on the lookout for newer and better plant varieties, be cautious about bringing them into your home. With new plants, follow the guidelines listed here and you'll be rewarded with healthy African violets.

Always isolate any new African violets you have bought from a garden center, nursery, or any store, regardless of their reputation. Even the plants your best friends give you as a gift need to go through this quarantine period. Keep new plants away from the others in your home. This allows you to watch the plants and carefully inspect them periodically for any signs of disease or insect problem. Consider treating the plants for insects once or twice during the quarantine period. Precautionary steps like this one may pay big dividends for you.

If a plant becomes noticeably sick during the two months of isolation, toss it in the garbage. Don't take any chances with these plants or you may lose many more. Any tools or utensils you use when working with a sick plant should be sterilized or disinfected chemically. Contaminated tools readily transfer diseases and insects to other African violets in your home. When

123

you work on a sick plant and then go to another part of the house to care for another plant, the tools will act as carriers for fungi and insects. Don't forget to wash your hands with hot water and soap to prevent the spreading of plant pests throughout your home.

Problems You May Create

Not all African violets die or have their beauty marred by disease or insects. One particular group of plant disorders is caused by improper cultural practices carried out by the plant's owners. Plant ailments of this kind are often referred to as ''physiological problems.'' Novice growers are more prone to these problems with their plants than are expert growers who have been working with African violets for years. Still, every grower needs to be alert to the possibility of a ''cultural disease'' striking the plants. Carelessness will surely lead to one or more problems. I would venture to say that over 90 percent of African violets which die, do so not because of a disease or insect pest but because of something the plant's owner did or did not do for it.

In other chapters we have already touched upon most of the various physiological problems which cause unhealthy African violets. For your convenience, I have listed each problem here so you will have a handy guide to check if your plants suddenly look sick. Study the symptoms each type of problem causes African violets to display. Commit some of these characteristic symptoms to memory so you can spot a problem when it develops. When you understand all these physiological problems, and what causes them, you'll have a much better chance to avoid these mistakes with your African violets.

List of Physiological Problems

Leaf Blotch

Plant Symptom

Your plant's leaves will suddenly display brownish blotches about one-eighth inch in diameter in size. The tissue in these areas will not regain any of its natural color again, and leaves will be left permanently marred.

The Cause and Its Cure

You are using water that is too cold. When watering your plants, water must be at room temperature before you use it. Fill a container with water and let it stand on the kitchen counter overnight prior to watering.

Incorrect Temperatures

Plant Symptom

Too Hot

Rapid plant growth, with stems and leaves which are soft, cause the leaves to droop over the edge of the pot. Flowers will not develop.

Too Cold

Having the temperature too cool causes plants to grow very slowly. A plant that fails to increase in size is the best indication of this condition. If you allow cool temperatures to persist, the leaves may begin curling up.

The Cause and Its Cure

Your failure to maintain the room in the ideal temperature range is the problem. Or maybe you have selected a location where it is impossible to modify the temperature to suit the African violets. The solution is to either move your plants, or adjust the temperature to 65 to 75 degrees F. At these temperatures your plants' vigor will be restored.

*Fluctuating
Temperatures*

Plant Symptom

A healthy plant will suddenly begin losing its flowers and dropping newly formed flower buds. Edges of the leaf margins may dry up, turn brown, and die.

The Cause and Its Cure

These symptoms suggest rapid changes in room temperature where the plants are being grown. This may be caused by the opening of an outside door and letting in a blast of cold winter air, or leaving a window open near the plants. The cure is to avoid putting the plants where they are exposed to drafts and changing temperature.

Low Humidity

Plant Symptom

The plant fails to produce blossoms of normal size; instead blossoms look more like miniature flowers and leaf margins will lose their green color and turn brown.

The Cause and Its Cure

Too little moisture in the air around the African violets is the culprit. Proper humidity is important to the overall health of the plants. Increase the humidity as much as possible by placing trays, filled with water, around your plants. Misting them also works, but don't overwet the plants.

Improper Feeding

Plant Symptom

Too Much

The plant will be growing too fast, developing deep-green leaves, and producing only a small number of flowers.

Too Little

Plant growth is very slow and plant parts (leaf and flowers) fail to reach the normal size of healthy plants. Leaves and stems lack good color, often look yellowish-green.

The Cause and Its Cure

In both cases it is a matter of giving the plants and improper diet. Set up a proper schedule for feeding your plants and stick to it. Usually a feeding once a month is all that the plants need.

If you have overfed them, do not apply a fertilizer until all the nutrients are used up from the soil and the plants return to normal. Avoid giving them a plant food high in nitrogen. The lack of sufficient plant food can be overcome by fertilizing twice a month until the plants recover.

Poor Lighting

Plant Symptom

Very few flowers, if any, will develop on the plant. The plant's new leaves will be small. Often the stems will become elongated, causing the leaves to look as if they are reaching up toward the light.

The Cause and Its Cure

These plants are showing the characteristic signs of receiving too little light. To overcome this problem, place the plants where they can get more light for a longer period of time. Consider the use of artificial lighting if it isn't possible to put your plants in a sunny spot in your home.

Excessive Light

Plant Symptom

Dark-green leaves curling over the rim of the pot as if trying to hide from light, leave margins may become scorched and turn brittle and unsightly, flowers lack their normal brilliance and look bleached and faded.

The Cause and Its Cure

Too much light causes these characteristics to develop in African violets. This usually occurs when the plants are placed in direct sunlight for too long. Shorten the amount of time the plants are in direct sunlight, or move them to a spot where they will be exposed to only filtered sunlight or artificial lighting.

Salt Buildup

Plant Symptom

Stems or petioles rot when touching the rim of the pot, reddish spots may appear on the stems, stems become limp, turn dark and mushy and cause the attached leaves to shrivel up and die.

The Cause and Its Cure

The white crust seen on soil-mixture surface and on the rim of the pot is caused by a buildup of salts. These salts come from the fertilizer and water you give the African violets. To reduce the chances of this problem occurring, leach water through the soil mixture to flush out the toxic salts. Periodically scrubbing the rims of the pots with steel wool, and plenty of fresh water, will also remove the salts. Another technique is to place aluminum foil or special rubber caps or wax on the rims of the pots.

Overwatering

Plant Symptom

Stems and leaves become limp (called wet wilt), turn mushy and then rot. Slow plant growth.

The Cause and Its Cure

Allowing the soil mixture to remain constantly moist is the cause of these symptoms. Watering too frequently, overwatering, plugged drain holes, improper bottom watering—all could cause the plants to die. Check water schedule and never water unless the soil surface is dry to the touch.

Underwatering

Plant Symptom

Leaf tips and leaf margins dry up, turn brown, and then die. Often the lower, older leaves will become yellow and drop off.

The Cause and Its Cure

Lack of water causes this problem. Be sure you are testing the soil moisture each day to determine if a plant needs water. Don't accidently skip a plant when you are routinely seeing to their water needs.

Plant Diseases

Fungi and viruses are the two types of disease organisms that will cause your plants the biggest problems. It can be very frustrating when your favorite African violet is looking absolutely gorgeous one day, and the next day its appearance is ruined by a disease. Fortunately, if you are following good cultural practices then the chances of a disease problem are greatly diminished. Isolation of all new African violets is an important procedure to follow in the prevention of disease problems.

Fungi belong to a low order in the plant kingdom. They are usually microscopic, unless they have infected a plant and a disease colony has developed. When the mass becomes large enough for you to see it, it is usually too late to save your African violet. Curing a plant once it is infected with a fungus may or may not be possible. Your safest bet is to toss the plant away as soon as you notice it is sick. Hopefully you will have gotten rid of it before the fungi spread to your other African violets.

There are literally thousands of different kinds of fungi that have been identified. You are probably most familiar with those which produce mushrooms and toadstools. You may even hunt the woods and moist pasture lands for the delicate morsels that are very tasty when sliced and fried in butter. So far as African violets are concerned, you need to know only a few different fungi and leave the rest for the mycologists to worry about.

Crown rot, gray mold, and powdery mildew are the three different fungi that show up most often in African violet circles. The first two are very serious pests. Powdery mildew is of less concern though it does pose a

COMMON FUNGI THAT ATTACK AFRICAN VIOLETS

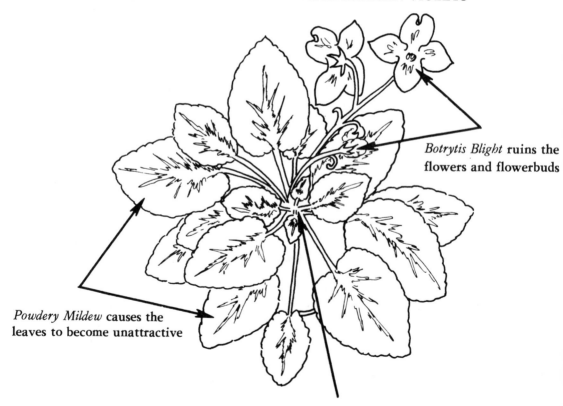

Botrytis Blight ruins the flowers and flowerbuds

Powdery Mildew causes the leaves to become unattractive

Crown Rot attacks at the heart of an African violet

problem for you and your plants. Let's take a look at each of the three fungi and become familiar with the general characteristics they display when attacking plants.

Crown Rot

One morning when you awaken, your African violets will look absolutely superb and flowering abundantly in all their glory. The leaves will be a rich green color and form a perfect rosette needed for a lovely show plant. Late in the afternoon you notice that a big change has occurred in the appearance of your favorite African violet. It has started to wilt, although you watered it at breakfast time. By evening the leaves are drooping over the edge of the pot, and the magnificent flowers are no longer standing high above the leaves of the plant.

Crown rot is the culprit! This disease is caused by getting the crown of the African violet wet, keeping the soil mixture too wet, and by watering your plants with water that is too cold.

When water is accidentally poured on the crown, you can take steps to prevent crown rot from infecting the plant. Softly blow on the crown to force

CROWN ROT DISEASE

Occasionally an African violet, which is not in need of water, will suddenly start drooping over the rim of the pot. When this happens suspect a fungus as the culprit.

the excess water to run off into the soil mixture. Air circulation across the crown also helps to evaporate the moisture from the surfaces of the plant.

The next step is to take soft tissue paper and wipe any remaining moisture from the crown. Be careful not to damage any leaves while drying the plants. Now gently blow again on the crown of the plant. All this blowing and wiping of moisture off the crown will help prevent crown rot from ever getting started. The best solution is to just be careful and avoid getting any water on the crown in the first place.

If you are able to accurately diagnose the problem in its early stages you may be able to save your favorite African violet, but you'll have to act quickly and repot it immediately after drying the plant's crown. Take the plant from its pot and remove all the soil mixture from the roots by washing them with warm water. Clip any dead roots and plant parts from the infected plants. Use a very porous soil mixture when repotting. This will help to insure good drainage and reduce the chances of crown rot infection. If you are lucky, the plant will survive and again produce lovely flowers.

Botrytis Blight

Gray mold may be another name by which you know this disease that attacks the delicate flowers and flower buds of an African violet. A flower or bud which becomes a mushy brown mass of tissue is infected with *Botrytis cinerea*. This fungus will attack when humidity is high and the temperature is too low. Entrance into a plant is usually through old flowers which have started to fade away due to old age or through dying leaves. For this reason it is important to remove any leaves or flowers when they have lost their beauty and started to die. Healthy plant parts are also subject to attack.

Avoiding this disease can be done by following a few simple plant-care procedures. Give the African violets plenty of room (don't crowd them too closely together) so there is good air circulation around them. When possible, avoid any conditions that lead to very high humidity around the plants when there is poor air circulation. Do not apply a nitrogen fertilizer in excessive amounts. Overfertilization with nitrogen makes it easier for fungus to attack African violets.

Even when following these procedures there is no guarantee that Botrytis Blight won't creep up on your plants. If it does, remove the infected parts as soon as you discover there is a "fungus-amongus" your African violets. As a further safety measure, spray the plants with one of the following fungicides (fungi killers): ferbam, captan, or thiram. It would be a good idea to isolate the sick plants until their health returns.

Powdery Mildew

African violet leaves that have a whitish-gray, dustlike appearance are

130

infected with an unusual fungus. Powdery mildew is not a serious disease so far as the health of the plant is concerned, unless you let it get completely out of control and fail to take any preventive measures to get rid of it. The changing of the nice green leaves to a whitish color ruins the appearance of African violets. To keep your plants looking nice and healthy, do something about the mildew.

The high humidity that favors the growth of the African violets is also favorable for the development of this disease. Good air circulation will help reduce the chance of mildew infection. Once the whitish fungus shows up on the leaves you can spray a chemical on the plant which will kill the mildew. Select either captan or acti-dione and liberally spray the surface of the leaves. This should rid your African violets of any powdery mildew present.

Viruses

These are the toughest diseases to diagnose. Most of the symptoms are identical to those caused by insects. Virus infections cause the leaves and flower petals to become streaked, leaves often become deformed, or you may just see yellowish spots occurring on them. Often the plant will appear to be in pretty good health, but it won't put forth any new growth or flowers when viruses are at work. All these symptoms may suggest that a virus infection is the problem, but usually it takes an expert to be sure. Whenever you are confident that a virus is definitely the problem, then just go ahead and toss the plant away. There are no known cures for a virus disease once it has a foothold on an African violet plant.

Insects do the best job of spreading viruses from one plant to another. Those which suck cell juices from the plant have been identified as the disease carriers. Three good examples of these types of insects are mites, leaf-hoppers, and aphids. Transferring a virus may also occur by using a cutting tool (razor, scissors, or a knife) on a virus-infected plant and then using the same utensil on a healthy African violet.

Controlling the virus itself is difficult to accomplish. Your best bet is to kill the vector (insect which is carrying the virus). This will help to prevent your plants from ever becoming infected. A good spraying program set up for your African violets will kill the insects and stop virus diseases dead in their tracks.

Those Bothersome Insects

No one likes to have bugs on the plants in their home, especially on prize African violets. Nothing is more shocking to avid gardeners than to be admiring their plants and suddenly see them come alive with little crawly bugs. You can avoid these problems by frequently inspecting your African violets. At least once a week look them over carefully and if you find any insects take the necessary steps to get rid of them. Leaving them alone allows them to increase in numbers until the insect population has grown enough to cause serious damage to the plants.

Infestation of insects often occurs when you use unsterilized soil mixtures or dirty pots for potting African violets. A second source of infestation is bringing new plants into the house without isolating them for two months from the rest of your plants. Many folks think that if they buy their plants from a greenhouse, gardening center, or a floral shop, that they'll be insect free. Not so! Such an assumption will cause you many headaches later when you are fighting a war with the bugs.

Getting rid of the insects is not a difficult job. Some old-fashioned home remedies may be the answer for you. If not, then read about controlling insects by using insecticides (bug killers). If only a few insects are present, use some tweezers and pick them by hand or use a soft brush to sweep them away. Alcohol on cotton dabs can be used to kill some insects. Just touch the alcohol soaked cotton dab to the pesty creature. The last home remedy is to

SIMPLE INSECT CONTROL

Two old fashioned solutions to insect problems that still have a place in today's gardening world.

Using tweezer to hand pick mealybugs.

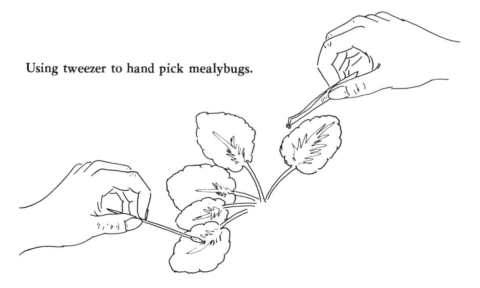

Alcohol soaked cotton dabs are an effective way to kill soft bodied insects such as aphids.

132

run faucet water in the kitchen sink until the temperature is constant and warm, hold the plant under the water and wash the insects down the drain. Be sure to keep the water from running onto the soil mixture.

Individual Pests

Aphids

These soft-bodied insects are black or green in color and are often inaccurately called plant lice by novice gardeners. Frequently aphids will produce a sweet substance called honeydew, which attracts ants. Aphids have the ability to reproduce easily.

Usually you will find these insects in clusters on the underneath side of leaves or on leaf stems. Aphids suck the juice from the plant cells. This causes the leaves to curl under and ruins the appearance of the plants.

Washing these pests off the plant with warm water is all that is usually necessary to get rid of them. For chemical control, there is a wide selection from which you can choose: nicotine sulfate, rotenone, malathion, diazinon, or pyrethrin sprays are available at most garden stores.

BE ON THE LOOKOUT FOR INSECT PROBLEMS

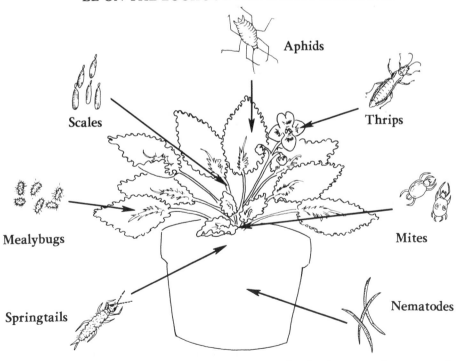

Arrows point out the location where each individual pest prefers to attack an African violet.

Mealybugs

Mealybugs feed on plant juices and cause serious injury to plants. You are dealing with two different types: one likes to feed on the roots of the plant, and the other prefers the underneath surface of the leaves or hides down in the leaf axil. Root-feeding mealybugs are fuzzy looking, almost as if they were covered with cotton. The airborne mealybugs are grayish-black in color and have a waxy coat. Both types are soft-bodied, oblong-shaped, slow-moving bugs which are closely related to scale insects.

Suspect mealybugs when the combined characteristic symptoms occur—leaves looking poorly and flower buds dropping off. These bugs may be very difficult to kill; it all depends on how mature they are when you spot them. Adult mealybugs are covered with a waxy coating which protects them very well; the young are easy to kill before they have a chance to form this protective barrier.

Chemical control will depend on whether you are dealing with the airborne type (on the leaf and crown) or the soilborne root feeders. Drench the soil mixture with malathion, diazinon, or systox to kill soilborne mealybugs. Treat airborne mealybugs according to the recommendations given for the non-chemical control of aphids. If this fails, then they can be killed by spraying the plants with malathion or diazinon.

Springtails

Little if any damage is done to African violets by this little pest. Less than one-eighth of an inch long, it is a slimy grayish insect found in the soil feeding on dead plant tissue. Probably your first encounter with this insect was when you were young and looking through stacks of old books or newspapers stored in a moist basement or garage. Their name, springtail, comes from their ability to jump great distances due to a springlike appendage on their bellies.

Soil sterilization is the best way to control this nuisance. Drenching the soil with an insecticide will also work.

Scales

Scale insects seldom become a problem with African violets, but if they show up you need to be able to identify them. Young scales crawl around very slowly, sucking juices from the plant. When mature, they attach themselves permanently to one spot and feed continuously on the plant. Adults are grayish or brown and reach up to three-sixteenths of an inch in length. Their general appearance looks very similar to that of a turtle which has pulled back into its shell.

Picking scales by hand when they are in the crawling stage works okay if there are only a few of them. You may also try washing them off with warm water before they become permanently attached to the plant surfaces. Malathion and diazinon may be sprayed on the infested plants for chemically controlling these pests.

Thrips

African violet growers have learned to dislike this pest immensely for it ruins the prettiest part of the plant. The damage caused by thrips is so upsetting because they cause flower buds to drop off (called bud blast), hence the flowers fail to pop up through the leaves.

One of the unseeable insects, thrips are so small you need a magnifying lens to find them. About the only way to really tell if they are present, other than by plant damage, is to knock them on a piece of white paper. They will appear as small dots scurring around trying to find a new hidding place.

Thrips are sucking insects which attack the leaves and delicate petals of blossoms. If the underneath portion of a leaf takes on a silvery appearance and the leaves eventually curl up, suspect thrips. Flower buds will wrinkle up, followed by collapsing of the bud stalk when thrips are at work. Should they attack a plant which has the flowers already open the petals will appear streaked or blotchy. Thrips also like to chew holes into the anthers of the flower, which allow the pollen grains to spill out on the flower petals. Pollen streaks on flower petals is a sure sign of active thrips working on a plant.

Treat your plant with malathion or sevin for control of this pest. You may try washing them off with some degree of success.

Other African Violet Pests

Not all pests of African violets belong to the insect family; some are from entirely different backgrounds in the animal kingdom. But it doesn't matter what their origin is if they are damaging your favorite plants. The worst offenders in this group of pests are mites, which are closely related to the spider family. Mites have eight legs and two body parts (head and abdomen); insects have six legs and three body segments (head, thorax, and abdomen).

Three distinct types of mites like to make African violets their home. They are the cyclamen mite, broad mite, and the red spider mite. All three can cause serious damage to African violets if the infestation is severe.

Cyclamen Mite

Many experts believe the cyclamen mite to be the most fearsome creature to ever attack African violets. It is too small to be seen with the naked eye and therefore is extremely hard to detect until it has gone to work on your plants. For this reason you need to be able to identify the different symptoms

African violets display when infested by cyclamen mites.

These tiny mites manifest themselves in four distinct phases of damage when attacking African violets. The infestation phase in which you first spot the mites is important to the overall health of the plants. Frequently cultural practices (lack of light, overwatering, etc.) which cause physiological problems are often confused with mite damage.

Phase I

Periodically pick up your plants and closely examine them, I'd say at least once every seven to ten days. Check the base of the individual leaves right where they are attached to the stems. A mite infested leaf will first turn yellowish or look water-soaked at the junction of leaf and stem. These leaves will either cease to grow or become deformed as they mature. Spot-checking your African violets to catch the cylcamen mite in this early infestation phase is an important step in keeping healthy plants.

Phase II

So you forgot to inspect the plants at regular intervals, and now you have noticed that a few of them are not looking well. On close scrunity you find that the center leaves of the rosette have ceased to grow and started to curl upward. The leaves are a light-green color now and dwarfed in size as compared to healthy leaves. In the final stages of this phase the leaves will have lost most of their beautiful green color and begun to shrivel up. At this stage the mites have severed the veins in the stems and food and water can no longer move into the leaves. Once this happens, phases III and IV occur rapidly.

Phase III

Leaves on your African violets are finally beginning to show the stress of the lack of food and water. They begin to turn brown after losing the green chlorophyll. Use a small magnifying lens for inspecting the hairs on the leaves of your plant. The hairs will be curled up in this phase of mite damage.

Phase IV

Now the crown of the African violet starts to become the victim of the cyclamen mites' appetite. The crown will turn brown and a few leaf stalk stubs will be barely visible. If the plant has reached this stage, you were either (a) on an extended vacation, (b) don't care about your plants, or (c) should have gotten some expert advice from another African violet grower. If you fit category (c) then, at the latest, Phase II is when you should have first sought some help.

A description of what is happening to the flower buds and blossoms was not included in the four phases of cyclamen mite infestation. Should your plant already have flower buds when the mites invade, the flowers will show the effect of the mites. As the buds open, blossoms will be deformed; the colorful petals may be missing or irregularly shaped; pistils and stamens may or may not be present either, and the stalk of the flower will become twisted and

136

look like a corkscrew.

Cyclamen mites are one of the main reasons why you should always follow the practice of isolating any new African violets before bringing them in with your other plants. During the isolation period, take some precautions to insure that if mites are present on the new plants that you don't transfer them to a healty plant. Mites will take a free trip on your hands and shirt-sleeves, so when working with isolated plants don't go directly to the other violets in your home. Spray the new plants three or four times with a mite killer during the isolation period. It can't harm the plant, and if mites are present it will help get rid of them.

I have said that the cyclamen mites are small and that a magnifying glass is needed to see them; but, really, how small are they? These mites are so minute in size that it would take literally hundreds of them placed in a single row to measure an inch long. Their size makes it difficult for even a trained eye to find them under a powerful microscope.

Mites prefer a hot, humid atmosphere in which to inflict their damage on African violets. Usually the younger, tender parts of the plant are subject to attack first. Mites tend to shy away from the older, tougher parts of the plant. Once mite damage has occurred, the plant parts affected are permanently deformed. Until new growth develops the plant should be moved to a spot where all your friends won't see it. Also, to protect other plants from mites, you want to isolate the infested plants.

Controlling Cyclamen Mites

Mites are difficult to kill because they are hidden in the center of the plant where they are protected by leaves and stems. It is hard to get insecticide down through the plant to where the mites are feeding. The hairs on the leaves also help stop the penetration of insecticide to the center of the plant.

Complete removal of a cyclamen mite-infested plant and burning it is a sure way to getting rid of this pest. Such drastic steps usually need not be taken; but if you go this route, then don't forget to get some cuttings and propagate new African violet plants for your collection. Be sure to dip the leave cuttings in a solution which contains a mite killer. Two or three dippings will insure a total kill of all the mites on the cuttings.

Dipping an entire plant while it is still in the pot is a good technique to use for cyclamen mite control. Do not immerse the soil mixture in the chemical solution. Prepare a mixture with kelthane, cythion, or demite, mixed in with water for dipping your African violets. Several immersions, spaced at one-week intervals, in this solution should do the job. This procedure should be followed until the new growth is no longer malformed. Once you have rid your African violets of cyclamen mites, you should consider scheduling a regular mite control treatment for your plants. Just plan on dipping the plants in the prepared solution once a month, and chances are excellent that you'll never see another cyclamen mite.

Spraying diazinon or demite on the infested plants will give a small measure of control of the mites. However, due to the inability of a solution to easily penetrate to the center of African violets this technique should not be your first choice.

Broad Mite

A whole lot needn't be said about this pest. Characteristic plant symptoms shown when a broad mite attacks is very similar to that of the cyclamen mite. Also the control measures for a broad mite are the same as those used on the cyclamen mite.

Minor differences between broad mites and cyclamen mites are apparent to a trained expert. The broad mite is very quick on its feet; cyclamen mites are very slow-moving. Broad mites feed on the underneath sides of the African violet leaves rather than deep down in the center of the plant. This makes the broad mite easier to kill because it is not as protected as its buddy, the cyclamen mite.

One symptom displayed by a broad mite-infested African violet is easy to recognize: the leaves will become distorted, curling down and over the edge of the pot. When these same leaves take on an unnatural shiny, silvery appearance then you'll know that the culprit is a broad mite.

Red Spider Mite

Although called a "spider," don't get the impression it is one. In reality it belongs to the same family as the cyclamen and broad mites. Like its close relatives, the red spider mite is extremely small and a magnifying lens is needed to see it. Another order of business which needs to be straightened out is the actual color of red spider mites. Contrary to their name, they come in a wide assortment of colors: red, green, yellow, brown, and black.

Red spider mite problems indicate that poor growing conditions exist where you have African violets. Check for proper relative humidity around the plants and see to it there is good air circulation around them. Exceedingly warm temperatures favor the growth of this pest. Often by just improving the growing conditions for the plants and washing them under a stream of warm water you can rid the plants of this pest.

These mites attack the underneath side of the leaves, sucking juices from the plant's cells and causing a speckled appearance and discoloration of the leaves. Leaves will turn whitish or bronze-looking, frequently accompanied by a very fine weblike netting similar in appearance to a spider web—hence the name spider mite. If left alone the red spider mite will multiply its ranks very quickly and the leaves of your African violets will go from the whitish, bronze stage to a yellowish color and eventually die and drop off one at a time.

Systemic chemicals work very well in the control of red spider mites.

138

Spread the granular chemical on the soil mixture and wash it into the soil. The roots will pick up the chemical and move it throughout the plants' plumbing system. When the mite sucks the juice from the plant cells it also gets a taste of the mite-killing chemical.

Nematodes

When an African violet looks sick, and you have tried all the old tricks to make it healthy and it hasn't responded, then consider the possibility of a nematode problem. These creatures are most often found in the soil (but not always) where they are feeding on the roots. They are very small, microscopic, wormlike creatures.

Nematodes cause the plants to loose their rich green color and turn them to a less desirable yellowish-green. This is due primarily to the inability of the infected roots to supply the plant with the necessary food to stay healthy.

Three ideas to keep in mind when thinking about nematodes are: 1) always sterilize any soil mixture you are going to use; this will kill any nematodes present; 2) keep your new African violets separated from the others until you are certain they are healthy; and 3) if you find nematodes in the soil mixture the best solution is to toss the plant in the garbage. But if the plant is very valuable, or you have a personal attachment to it, there are chemicals you can use to kill the nematodes.

Examine the roots for definite proof of the presence of this pest. Swollen nodules, usually referred to as galls, will appear on the roots if nematodes are causing any problems. Galls on the roots indicate that you need to treat the soil mixture with a chemical if you aren't going to toss the plant away. Drenching the soil mixture with either nemagon (DD) or mylone should kill the nematodes. These chemicals are dangerous to handle, so read the labels and be extremely careful.

Medicine Cabinet for African Violets

It is difficult to discuss specific chemicals for use in controlling pests. The difficulty is not in knowing which chemical will control what pest, but in anticipating which chemical the government is suddenly going to decide on removing from the counter. Some excellent pesticides have been removed from garden centers because of some rather arbitrary decisions reached by some government agency filled with lawyers who know very little about pesticides.

Pesticides have been receiving a bad rap ever since Rachel Carson's book, *Silent Spring*, startled the world and started the ecology groups using the same scare tactics. To put things in a little better perspective, let's consider some of the things that happen in your home. What about those household chemicals and cleaners you use everyday, then wash down the sink? Out of sight, out of mind? Yet they end up in the nearest river, and cause pollution, killing the wildlife. Disinfectants, bathroom cleaning products, hair sprays, detergents, and so on and on — all are as deadly as any pesticide.

Even if you were to dump small amounts of pesticides down the drain (which I certainly don't recommend) they wouldn't be as big a problem as the household products that go into a river. The difference is purely psychological. One is labeled as a killer, and you are told to worry about it. The other is labeled as a helpful household cleaning product, or whatever, but you don't worry about it harming any living creatures. Yet both are killers when you tip up a bottle of either one and take a drink.

But don't let the thought of using a pesticide scare you away from the job if your African violets need to be debugged. More people are injured in cars, in home accidents, at work, and while participating in sports than ever become ill handling pesticides. Still it is important to handle pesticides with extreme caution. Read the labels and follow the directions carefully and you will have no problems applying pesticides.

Selecting the correct pesticide is the first chore you are faced with. To do this, you must properly identify the pest you want to get rid of. After identifying the pest, it is important to understand its living habits. Where does it live? How does it feed on the plant? When is it most susceptible to chemical control? Answers to these questions will help you choose the proper pesticide. If you are in doubt, check with the salesman at a reputable garden center or nursery. He is trained to be able to answer your questions. *Never* be afraid to ask a question when selecting pesticides.

The following list of pesticides are safe for use on African violets. This list is by no means a complete one, but may be used as a reference point for a solution to some of your pest problems.

Pesticides

Cygon	Malathion	Pyrethrin
Cythion	Mylone	Rotenone
Demite	Lindane	Sevin
Diazinon	Negagon (DD)	Sodium selenate
Isotox	Nicotine sulfate	Systox
Kelthane		

10
Light and Your Plants

In this chapter you will be introduced to how light, natural and artificial, causes African violets to produce those gorgeous plants you so thoroughly enjoy. Part of the fun of growing plants is being aware of how nature governs the life of a plant. This will allow you to understand the cultural practices you follow in caring for your favorite African violets.

Now don't stop with this paragraph and say to yourself that you aren't interested. Read on, and you'll learn how plants are the only living organisms able to convert light energy into chemical energy for the manufacturing of food. The reason why some houseplants can get by on very little light, and others shrivel up and die, will be explained to you. The secret of why the leaves of an African violet are green or reddish, and the flowers appear in red, blue, purple, and all sorts of colors, will be revealed. The mystery of why some plants flower only in the spring and others in the fall is also solved for you in this chapter.

Some very complicated principles of plant growth and development as affected by light will be touched on. But don't worry, I don't plan on getting lost in any long detailed discussions on these subjects. My plan is to let you enjoy each new topic while you learn about the inner workings of what makes African violets tick.

You already know that all plants need light in order to live. Light is important to plants in many different ways for their normal day-to-day functions. It is the mechanism that triggers the production of food (called photosynthesis) in all plants. Without light, the earth would be a barren desert. Plant characteristics such as size, stem elongation, flower formation, seed germination, and color of the plant all come under the influence of light. Therefore anyone interested in growing plants needs to have a knowledge of how the light affects a plant's development and growth. This is especially true for African violets because of their sensitivity to the amount of light they need to stay beautiful.

141

What Is Light?

Light is a nebulous form of matter that shines on the earth from sunrise to sunset everyday of the year. The dictionary defines light as a mass of energy which travels in wavelike patterns at 186,000 miles per second and makes sight possible. The wavelength characteristics of light are very important, as you will find out later. Light is mostly a sensation your eyes feel but do not see much of. You can see only a small portion of the different wavelengths of light before it strikes an object. The light you perceive is in the form of the colors reflected from the surface of these objects. For instance, a sunset is caused by the reflection of light off the dust particles floating in the atmosphere.

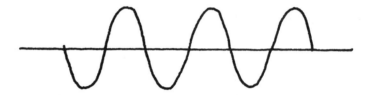

Light travels at a speed of 186,000 miles per hour in wavelike patterns. It is generally accepted that nothing in the universe can ever exceed the speed of light.

Colors You See

Have you ever wondered why the leaves of a plant are green? Or why a poinsettia has those beautiful red bracts you enjoy every Christmas season? What about the purples, blues, pinks, yellows and all the other colors found in nature? All the beautiful colors plants display are due to the light they absorb and reflect.

The sun emits radiant energy or light. Just as there are different kinds of cars, so are there different kinds of light. Quality of the light is measured by the varying types of light that reach the plant. The light or radiant energy is divided according to the length of individual light rays or wavelengths. Some are short, and others are very long. These divisions of light make up a color spectrum which allows the sun's light energy to be handily classified. This classification will give us a simple approach for discussing a very complicated subject.

In your beginning biology or physics class in school the use of a prism was most likely discussed. Its use in determining the sunlight's energy or color spectrum has been known for many years. If a beam of light passes through a prism the different wavelengths of the light are bent or separated by differing degrees according to the individual length of the light rays or wavelengths. The results are seen as various colors, called the visible color spectrum. Other wavelengths of light go beyond either end of the visible spectrum but they are of little importance to a plant's development.

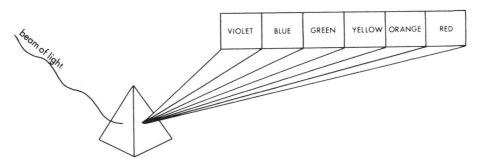

As light passes through the prism the individual wavelengths are dispersed, forming the visible color spectrum. It is these colors the eye is able to perceive.

The visible spectrum, then, is the light reflected to your eye in the form of the various colors you use. In the case of an African violet, the flower appears to be purple because of the light reflected off the flower to your eye.

A very small unit of measurement must be used to explain the length of the sun's individual light rays. The unit of measurement used is called an angstrom. It would take 250 million angstroms to equal the more familar inch to which you are accustomed. The table below shows the various colors created by different wavelengths of sunlight and the length of each one.

Visible Light Spectrum

Color	Length in Angstroms*
Violet	3,900 - 4,200
Blue	4,200 - 4,900
Green	4,900 - 5,400
Yellow	5,400 - 5,900
Orange	5,900 - 6,500
Red	6,500 - 7,600

*Since 250 million angstroms equal one inch, 100,000 violet wavelengths placed end to end would be slightly over an inch in length.

There is no need to try to commit this visible color spectrum to memory. Let this table be your handy reference whenever you need to use the information. The purpose of explaining the different wavelengths and the color they produce is so that in later discussions you can readily see how light plays an important role in the color of your plants and in the other plant development processes.

The human eye is unable to detect light until it is reflected off an object, then it is easily distinguished in all its various colors. The various colors plants display depend on the types of pigments contained in the leaves. One pigment, chlorophyll, absorbs all the light but that which is green. This part of the light is reflected to your eye and causes the leaves to look green to you.

Plant structures and leaves of plants which are not green, absorb the green light and reflect other colors to your eyes. For example, a reddish-purple leaf of a dwarf plum tree is high in anthocyanin and caroteniod pigments. All you need to know about these two pigments is that both absorb green and yellow light, and reflect the red and blue light, thus causing the leaves to be reddish-purple. This same principle holds for the red and purple blossoms of the African violets you enjoy so much.

THE COLORS YOU SEE IN PLANTS

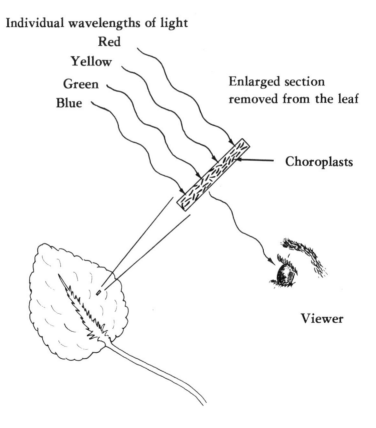

Individual wavelengths of light
Red
Yellow
Green
Blue

Enlarged section
removed from the leaf

Choroplasts

Viewer

As the various wavelengths of light strike a leaf some are absorbed, while others are not. In the case of an African violet leaf the red, yellow, and blue wavelengths are absorbed for the photosynthesis process. The green wavelengths are reflected to the eye, causing the viewer to see a green leaf.

The various pigments found in plants—chlorophyll, carotenoids, xanthophylls, anthocyanin—are responsible for the various colors you see in plants. These pigments are not the colors themselves but they have the ability to absorb the different wavelengths of light and thus control what light is then reflected to your eyes.

How Your Plants Use Light

Light plays many roles in the life of all plants. The most important one being in the photosynthesis of food for the plant. Light also enters into many other plant functions as a regulatory process. A good example of this is the opening and closing of flowers in certain species of plants.

You are probably very familiar with one such plant—your friend the dandelion. Observe it on an overcast day when the light is very weak and you'll notice that most of the yellow flowers are folded up. But if the sky is clear and the sun is beaming strongly on your lawn, the dandelions present will open up and expose the yellow flowers that mar the appearance of your lawn.

Four-o'clocks, found in many a gardener's flowerbeds, react to light just the opposite of dandelions. In a dim or weak light, flowers of the four-o'clocks will be magnificently displayed. Let the sunlight become too bright, and the flowers fold up and wait for the evening hours when the sunlight is dim again. This response of the plant's flowers to the light is called photonastic.

Food Production in Plants

Photosynthesis occurs in green plants whenever light strikes the plant's surface. Of all the light that reaches the earth from the sun, only 1 percent is absorbed by green plants. The other 99 percent is absorbed either by the earth and water or reflected back into the atmosphere. This very small portion of sunlight used by plants is the basis for all life on this planet.

The actual percentage of light absorbed by a plant depends on the thickness of the leaves. The thicker the leaves, the more light they will absorb. This principle is very important in selecting plants for use in your home. Household plants with thick succulent leaves can do very well in the dim light present in most homes. This is why tropical plants do so much better in your home than many other types of household plants.

Just how does light enter into this process of photosynthesis?

It all begins when light is absorbed by specialized structures, called chloroplasts, which are found in the cell sap of all green plants. The green-colored pigment is referred to as chlorophyll. One square inch of leaf surface may contain close to one billion chloroplasts filled with chlorophyll. It is this green pigment that stains children's clothing when they slide across the grass on a lawn. The crushed plant cells allow the chlorophyll to ooze out on

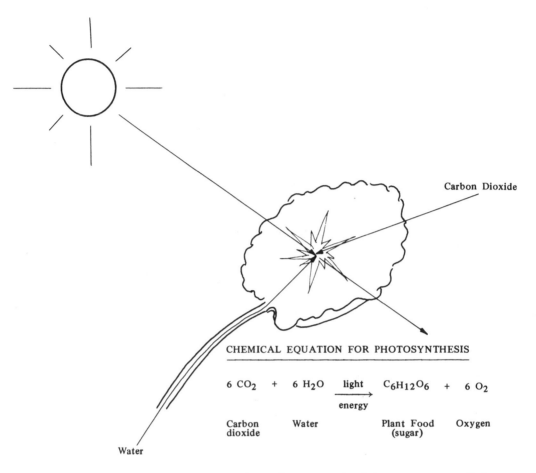

CHEMICAL EQUATION FOR PHOTOSYNTHESIS

$$6\ CO_2\ +\ 6\ H_2O\ \xrightarrow[\text{energy}]{\text{light}}\ C_6H_{12}O_6\ +\ 6\ O_2$$

| Carbon dioxide | Water | Plant Food (sugar) | Oxygen |

African violets are able to produce their own food by a process called *photosynthesis*. This complicated plant function occurs in the leaf where the water and carbon dioxide are broken up by the light's energy. The individual units are then recombined to form the plant food African violets need for healthy growth and elegant blossoms.

the children's clothing.

As the light is being absorbed by the plant, two other elements are entering the plant. Carbon dioxide (a gas) is absorbed through the leaves while water is moving up through the roots toward the leaves. When you have water and carbon dioxide in the presence of light, a series of chemical reactions occur in the leaf which convert these elements into the food energy needed by plants. This total process of food manufacturing is then referred to as photosynthesis.

Light Influences Flowering

Light and its control over when plants will flower is an interesting phenomenon you should know about. Once you understand just exactly how light controls flowering, you will know one of the secrets that mystifies most gardeners and African violet hobbyists.

Back in 1920 two United States Department of Agriculture scientists, W. W. Garner and H. A. Allard, discovered the secret of how light controls flowering in plants. Their discovery was the key to unlocking new horizons to botanists, horticulturalists, and home gardeners. The effect of light on the development of flowering and vegetative growth of plants is called photoperiodism.

The structure in a plant's leaf which is responsible for the phenomenon of photoperiodism is called phytochrome. This body is activated by light, and releases chemicals that cause flower buds to begin growth. The bright red wavelengths found in light appear to be the most active in causing the phytochrome body to give up its flower-making chemicals.

Flowering of plants varies considerably in nature. Many plants flower only in the spring, others prefer the fall, and some plants seem to want to flower all the time. The reason for this strange behavior in plants is tied in with the amount of light they need to produce flowers. Spring flowering plants require only ten to twelve hours of light daily for the phytochrome to release its flower forming chemicals. Fall flowering plants require fourteen to sixteen hours of daily light before they'll begin to display any flowers for your enjoyment.

Allard and Garner found that plants could be divided into three distinct groups according to their light needs to induce flowering. The categories are short day, long day, and indifferent.

A microscopic view into the cells of an African violet leaf would reveal specialized structures called *phytochromes*. When light strikes these cells they release a flower forming hormone. This hormone moves from the cells to the base of the leaf stem, causing new blossoms to develop.

147

Short Day

Plants in this group require ten to twelve hours of light a day to produce flowers. Examples: Chrysanthemums, cockscomb, cosmos, kalanchoe, poinsettias, cocklebur, soybean, begonia, salvia, Christmas cactus, true violets, forsythia, marigold, globeamaranth, zinnia, morning glory, lamb's quarters, ragweed, corn, and most asters and goldenrod.

Long Day

Fourteen to sixteen hours of light will cause flowers to form. Examples: Tuberous begonias, spinach, petunia, aster, calceolaria, sugar beets, digitalis, iris, bachelor's button, forget-me-nots, phlox, rudbeckia, lettuce, gladiolus, hollyhock, radish, verbena, barley, garden beets, and China asters.

Indifferent

This particular group of plants hasn't any specific daylight hours required for flowering. As you will see in the chapter on lighting needs of African violets, the number of flowers these plants produce will vary according to the amount of light they receive. Examples: African violets, roses, tomatoes, four-o'clocks, garden beans, tobacco, vetch, calendula, zinnias, cyclamen, nasturtium, snapdragons, carnations, and your friend the dandelion. Unfortunately many weedy plants fall into this category, making them prolific seed producers and difficult to completely eliminate.

Understanding the role light plays in a plant's life is an important step toward becoming an expert on growing African violets. Although some of the ideas presented in this chapter may seem to be unrelated to growing African violets, you will see how to use this information in Chapter 12, Growing African Violets Under Lights.

Natural Light for Your African Violets

The lack of sufficient light causes plants to develop weak, spindly stems, small dark-green leaves and flower production will be just about nil. On the other hand, too much light can be harmful to African violets. If the light is too bright or intense the plants will turn a yellow, bleached-out color and leaf edges will dry up and slowly turn brown.

For these reasons the window locations where the plants will be grown must be selected with care. Check the amount of sunlight coming through each window. Is it direct, or filtered light? How bright is it? Light that filters through tree leaves to a windowsill is usually an excellent choice for African violets, especially in a west or east window in the summertime.

Don't let friends lead you into believing that African violets can never be grown in full sunlight. They can, but it all depends on the time of the year. During early spring, late fall and winter months, direct light from the sun, if for only a few hours a day, will be very beneficial to the growth of the African violets. The hotter, brighter sunlight of the summer is not good for plants; it will burn the foliage and cause ugly brown blotches to appear on them.

Which windows are best for growing African violets? It depends on the time of year. For year-round locations, north and east windows provide the best lighting. A north window is okay for the three summer months, but after that the plants should be relocated to other windowsills. The south windows of your home are okay for the short winter days, or if only filtered light comes through in the summer.

There is a simple test for determining if the light is too bright for an African violet. Run your hand between the plant and the sunlight. If you can just barely see a shadow cast on the plant then the light is just right. A clearly defined, heavy shadow indicates that the sunlight is too strong and the plant should be moved.

When growing African violets in a windowsill planter, all the light reaching the plants will be coming from the same direction. If you overlook this fact your plants will respond by growing more on the side from which the light comes. This causes the plants' growth to become lopsided if you don't take steps to correct the problem. Overcome this by periodically turning the African violets so a new side is continually exposed to the light. A quarter turn of the pot once a week, say on a Friday morning, will do the job. Rotating African violets on a regular schedule keeps them growing uniformly and enhances their appearance.

11
Artificial Lighting

Plants do very well in the natural lighting when being grown out-of-doors or in a sunny spot in your house, but with the use of artificial lighting you are no longer restricted to growing African violets on windowsills where they get plenty of sunshine each day. With the use of artificial lighting, your plant growing horizons can move to places always thought of as the "dark corners" of your home. The attic, basement, or bookcases are dimly lit spots which can be turned into African violet havens through the use of artificial lights.

Artificial lighting has been used to grow plants in some rather unusual places on this earth. Researchers working within a few thousand feet of the South Pole grew a vegetable garden, under lights, eight hundred feet beneath the ice, snow, and blustery weather of the Antarctic. In another unique situation the versitale sailors of the U. S. Naval Submarine Force undertook the task of growing plants in the very depths of the oceans. The men of the *Polaris* submarine force remain submerged for months and have been able to supplement their diets with fresh vegetables by having an understanding of artificial light and how to use it to meet the needs of the various vegetables they were growing.

Thomas A. Edison, while staying in his winter home at Fort Myers, Florida, perfected the first light bulb in his laboratory in 1879. Strangely enough, the filament of his first light bulb was made from the bamboo plant. Mr. Edison was also responsible for the development of the fluorescent lamps common in today's homes and offices. The lighting of a room at a flick of a switch was one of this man's great dreams which became a reality for millions. Little did he realize the importance his inventions would have on plant growers around the world.

Some of the earliest known work using artificial lighting for growing plants was done by L. H. Bailey in 1893. He was interested in studying the effect of ultraviolet light rays on plant growth. In his studies he used a miner's carbon arc lamp, enclosed in glass. This prevented the ultraviolet

150

rays from damaging the plants since these longer wavelengths of light cannot pass through glass. This is the same principle that prevents sunburn when you are in your car on a hot summer afternoon.

Bailey's early work demonstrated that artificial lighting was very beneficial to plants. In his writings he referred to it as "electro-horticulture." Research continued slowly for the next twenty years, but very little interest was shown toward this new technique for growing plants. It was the discovery of photoperiodism (the effect of the length of daylight on flowering in plants) by Allard and Garner which finally stirred everyone's interest in manipulating the length of the days to improve plant development. Scientists finally understood the importance of this new principle and realized the profound effect it would have on agriculture.

Giant steps were taken in research and the use of the concept in greenhouses for commercial flower growing. By late 1950s and early in 1960 the use of artificial lighting was becoming commonplace. Everyone involved in horticulture knew of the principles involved, and most were actively engaged in using artificial lighting in some way. Today it is not uncommon for plants to be grown totally under artificial lighting.

Phytoillumination is the term scientists have coined for growing plants under lights. By breaking down this term into its fundamental parts we see that phyto- means plants and -illumination means lighting.

The advantages of phytoillumination are obvious. When you are using artificial lights for growing African violets you need not be concerned with whether the sun will or will not come out from behind the clouds. This gives the plants a feeling of being free and no longer tied to nature's apron strings. African violets grown under lights are able to reach a peak of perfection not possible under conditions of natural sunlight.

Growing African violets under lights is very important to city dwellers. Many buildings are so close together it is impossible to grow healthy plants without the aid of lights. The interested African violet fanciers who use artificial lighting are usually the envy of all their neighbors. They will have beautiful African violets and everyone will wonder what the secret is.

Spot-O-Sun Grow-Lite   Ripe-N-Gro Sun-Lite

Two popular table lamps, with round agricultural fluorescent tubes, provide a nice display for African violets in the home. *Courtesy of Indoor Gardening Supplies.*

Lights That Suit Your Plants

If you are planning on using artificial lighting for growing African violets, you should have some knowledge of the different types of lighting fixtures available. You may choose from the following: incandescent, fluorescent, neon, mercury vapor, mercury fluorescent or agriculture lamps. For household use your best bets are the incandescent, fluorescent and agriculture lamps. Your knowledge of these three types of light fixtures is important so you can pick the one that best fits your particular needs.

Incandescent Lighting

Everyone is familiar with this type of light. It is the standard filament light bulb found in almost every lamp in use today. Do you know how it produces light? The principle is very simple. The filament bulb contains two wires which are connected by a single tungsten wire. When a switch is turned on, the electric current is allowed to flow from one wire to the other across the tungsten wire bridge. As this happens, the tungsten wire becomes heated to an extremely high temperature (4,000 to 5,000 degrees F.) until it begins to glow. This creates the light emitted from the bulb. Because of the large amount of heat produced in this process you must be careful when using an incandescent lighting system. The heat can easily damage or kill African violets.

To overcome this heat problem special incandescent bulbs have been developed. These new bulbs have built-in reflectors which reduce the amount of heat that will reach the plants below. The reflector actually conducts the heat up and away, reducing the temperature at the plant's surface by as much as 60 to 70 percent, enough so as not to harm the tender African violets. This type is called a cool-beam incandescent light bulb.

Incandescent light contains a very high percentage of red and far-red light waves which are very important if you are to have magnificent flowering African violets. However, there is too low a percentage of blue light waves for good food production in plants.

Usually incandescent lights are not used alone in an artificial lighting setup. The problem of an imbalance of proper light rays, heat buildup and the expense of using them are the reasons most often cited. The new fluorescent and agriculture lamps offer a better way to set up a lighting system.

The use of incandescent lights in combination with fluorescent lights is common practice. Each helps to overcome the disadvantages of the other. A proper ratio of light emitted from each is important to the health of African violets. This will give the plants the quality of light they need for excellent growth and maximum flower production. Let's look into the different features of fluorescent lights before finishing this topic of proper ratio of light when incandescent and fluorescent lights are used together.

152

Fluorescent lights are excellent to use when growing African violets under artificial lights. The light produced is of high intensity (brightness) which is great for plant growth. This brightness is also terrific for photosynthesis of food to meet the plants' needs. The quality of the light (color) emitted by fluorescent lights duplicates the sunlight very well. The light is weak in red rays which are so important to flowering in African violets. This is why the use of incandescent lighting (produces red rays) with fluorescent lights is suggested.

Advantages of the fluorescent lights are numerous. They are very economical when it comes to producing light. For the amount of money you spend, the fluorescent light's efficiency in converting electrical energy into light energy is three times greater than that of the incandescent bulb; plus the light is more evenly distributed as it is emitted from a fluorescent light. Heat given off is so minimal that African violets can easily be grown within four or five inches of the fluorescent light bulbs.

Beautiful African violets can be grown under fluorescent lights. This set up works nicely for use in small areas. *Courtesy of the Floralite Company.*

As a fluorescent light ages it gives off less light. The average lifespan is 7,500 to 12,000 hours before the tubes need to be replaced. It is not uncommon for fluorescent lights to be only half as bright at the end of 7,000 to 10,000 hours of actual use. One way to overcome this lower light intensity is to move the lights down closer to the plants. But when you do this, the plants on the edges of a lighted bench will suffer from the effects of having less light reaching them. A better solution is to simply replace the lamps once a year. If you have left the lights on for twelve hours a day, this means that you have gotten 4,380 hours use out of them. While there is still plenty of good light being emitted, early replacement on a yearly schedule insures that your African violets are always given the best possible lighting for maximizing their beauty.

The table below, condensed from the United States Department of Agriculture Miscellaneous Publication No. 879, shows the effect of age on the amount of light fluorescent tubes emit after being used for only a short period of time.

Distance From Lamps (inches)	Four Lamps	
	Used*	New
6	820	1,000
12	480	600
18	320	420

*Used approximately 200 hours

Two hundred hours is really a very short period in the length of time you expect to use a fluorescent tube when you first install it in a lighting setup. It only represents between fourteen to twenty days when the lights are in use from ten to fourteen hours a day.

Don't overlook the importance of replacing the fluorescent tubes on a regular basis. Beautiful plants must have proper light intensities to live up to their reputation of producing blossoms year-round.

When you go to buy a replacement tube for your artificial lighting setup be prepared for the salesman to ask you what type tubes you want: cool-white, warm-white or daylight tubes. Confusing? It needn't be. Just answer the question simply by stating that you prefer a cool-white fluorescent tube, then you will be sure you are getting the type lamp that emits the proper light for growing healthy African violets.

Agricultural Lamps

After several years of using incandescent and fluorescent lights, researchers were able to conclude that these lights did not emit the correct balance of light required to produce all-around healthy plants. They were either too high in blue light and too low in red light, or vice versa. During this same period of time the incandescent bulbs were not in favor because of the heat they created.

To overcome this problem a new, special type of light source was developed especially for growing plants indoors under lights. These special lights were called agricultural lamps and may be bought under a wide variety of brand names. Three popular ones are Gro-Lux, Plant Gro, and Plant Lite. The advantage of using these lights is that they do not have to be used in conjunction with incandescent bulbs. These special lamps emit an increased proportion of red while the blue light, and the amount of yellow and green

154

light, is reduced. This gives a more balanced light. The cost of these special lights is more than that of the fluorescent tubes, but the ability of plants to use more of the light emitted offsets the cost.

The visual effect of these lights is enough to attract everyone's attention. Because of the larger proportion of blue and red light, these agricultural lamps radiate a purplish-rose glow which some gardeners feel adds much to the beauty of their plants. For this reason you may wish to use the colors produced by these lights to enhance the decor of your home.

African violets look absolutely magnificent when grown under these lights. The brilliant colored light causes the African violet's natural colors to become vivid — reds are redder, greens become deeper green, and the blossoms are turned into crown jewels. Removal of plants from under these lights causes them to appear as they normally would in natural light. Some African violet growers argue that the plants should not be grown under agriculture lamps because of the unnatural appearance the light sheds on the plants. I don't agree with this argument. Do whatever you can to improve the health of your African violets, and if it also enhances their beauty at the same time then you are getting more for your money and efforts.

Balanced Lighting

Reference to using balanced lighting for healthy plant growth has been made several times. Let's take the time now to look at what balanced lighting means and how to achieve it through the use of artificial lighting.

Plants grow and flower best when the light they receive is rich in blue and red light rays. Photosynthesis (food production) in plants is at its best when blue light is available to the plants. Flowering is dependent on the amount of red light available. Balanced lighting, then, refers to having the blue and red light in proper proportions to each other so as to satisfy a plant's requirements and your desire for beautiful blossoms.

Incandescent bulbs are rich in red light rays, which stimulate the growth and development of the flowering. If incandescent light is all you use in your artificial lighting setup the plants would eventually lose their health due to inadequate food production.

Fluorescent lights emit strong blue light rays along with a small amount of red light. For this reason African violets will do okay for quite a while under these lights but in the end they will suffer. Flowering is usually the first thing to stop developing; then the vegetative growth ceases.

To overcome this problem of balanced lighting, use fluorescent and incandescent bulbs together in the same light setup for your African violets. This will give the plants the necessary blue and red light rays for healthy growth. The ratio of blue to red light is important to African violets. Too much or too little of either light ray is not good. Use one thirty watt incandescent bulb per eighty watts of fluorescent light. Agricultural lamps come close to emitting the proper balance of red and blue light. For this reason African violets do extremely well when grown under these rose colored lights.

To make sure you really understand the importance of giving your African violets balanced lighting consider this fact for a moment: An African violet plant, when grown under proper lighting, will produce 50 percent more blossoms for your enjoyment. Taking this statement into consideration, you can easily see how light plays a key role in the life of an African violet and how well it performs for you.

Brightness of Light Important

You can easily judge light intensity (brightness) because of the sensitivity of your eyes to light. They are excellent gauges of the sun's ability to release energy in the form of light; however, all you can tell is whether the light is too bright, too dark or just right for your needs. Unfortunately a plant's needs are not the same as yours, so you should be able to measure the light someway to find out its exact intensity.

Probably the most familiar instrument for measuring the brightness of light is a light meter used to obtain the proper settings on cameras. These meters are not too expensive and are accurate enough for measuring light intensity for African violets. The readings of the brightness of the light are expressed in terms of footcandles. Twenty footcandles of light is not as strong as 500 footcandles of light.

Remember that light meters only check for the brightness of light and do not help in determining if the light is properly balanced for good plant growth. It is possible to obtain a high reading in footcandles and still have a plant suffering from lack of proper lighting.

Let's get off the subject of artificial lighting for a moment and look into the natural intensity of sunlight. Just how bright is sunlight at various times of the year? Well, it will vary according to where you live, whether you are inside or outside, or which window in the house you are interested in checking as a possible location for your African violets. On a hot summer day when the sun is directly overhead, light intensities of 10,000 footcandles have been recorded. Pick a cloudy December day and you may get a reading on your light meter as low as 500 footcandles.

During the winter the amount of light entering your windows varies according to the side of the house in which they are located. Obviously a south window will have the strongest sunlight, and the north windows the least. At the north windows you may get a reading of 125 to 250 footcandles at noon; the east and west windows should be approximately 250 to 500 footcandles of light shining through. In a south window it is not uncommon to get readings as high as 5,000 footcandles during the brightest time of the day.

156

The readings given here hold only if you live in a line somewhere between Salt Lake City, Utah and New York City. Below this imaginary line your readings will be higher, and above it you can expect lower readings.

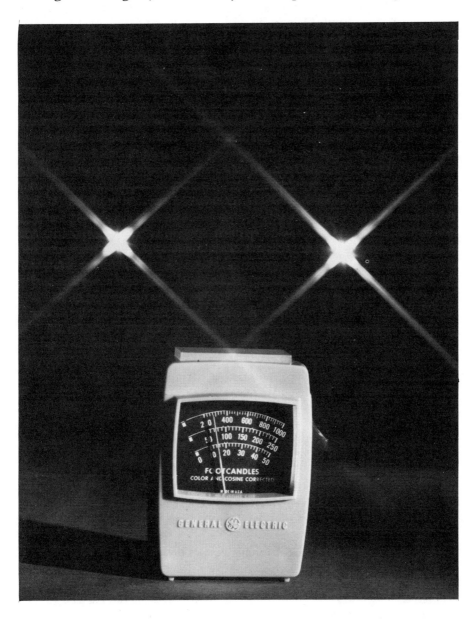

A general purpose light meter is a handy gardening tool for checking the brightness of the light shining on the African violets. These lovely plants will produce outstanding blossoms when a reading of 400 to 650 foot candles is registered. *Courtesy of General Electric.*

As the sun moves north and the days get longer the sun's intensity is also increasing. Along our imaginary line across the United States the sunlight intensity, out-of-doors, will reach 7,000 footcandles in the early spring, 8,000 in late spring, and on June 21 (longest day of the year) you may obtain a reading of 10,000 footcandles.

Natural Day Length

City	Hours of Daylight	
	June 21	Dec. 21
Seattle, Washington	16	8½
St. Paul, Minnesota	15¾	8½
Washington, D.C.	15	9½
San Francisco, California	14¾	9¾
Dallas, Texas	14½	10
Miami, Florida	13¾	10½

Fall time sees the light intensity drop back down as gradually as it went up. Indoor light intensities are considerably less, especially during the winter months. As you move into the house away from the windows, light intensity may drop to as low as 20 to 30 footcandles on an overcast day. This is especially true for the east, west and north windows where sunlight isn't shining directly through the windows.

For reading this book, twenty footcandles of light is sufficient to prevent eye strain. This amount of light does not meet the minimal requirements of most houseplants. Usually the figure of 50 footcandles is considered the bare minimum; any lower than this and the plants will suffer. At 100 to 300 footcandles African violets will grow rapidly, produce healthy leaves and develop some flowers. Increase the light intensity up to 400 to 650 footcandles and you'll see a tremendous increase in the number of flowers produced by the African violets. Keep in mind that flowering is controlled by two factors—light intensity and day length. Both factors will be looked at closely in the next chapter.

Obtaining these proper light intensities is not a problem when growing African violets under artificial lights. All you have to do is take a reading to determine the footcandles of light falling on your plants. If the reading isn't as high as it should be you can move the lights closer to the African violets or simply add another light fixture to your setup.

12

Growing African Violets Under Lights

*A*s an African violet grower you should try growing your plants under artificial lights. Once you've tried it, I doubt you'll return to growing all your plants on a windowsill. What's that? You don't have a place in the house for such an adventure? Everyone has at least one spot where artificial lighting can be used. Look around, find a spot, and give it a try. If you do, your African violets will be the envy of all your friends in a few short months.

More is known about growing African violets under artificial lights than about any other single plant. African violets are extremely fond of the soft colors of fluorescent lights. Their ability to grow so beautifully and flower so profusely under artificial lighting is one of the primary reasons why African violets are the most popular flowering houseplant today.

Growing African violets under artificial lights intensifies all their natural colors. Green leaves become jadelike in their appearance. Normal light-pink blossoms become a brilliant pink. Your plants will become so beautiful you will be very hesitant to ever again return to growing them under natural light.

Many African violet fanciers, who have discovered the joys of using artificial lighting, rotate their plants around the house placing them under the lights for brief periods to restore the brilliance the plants lost when placed in natural sunlight. Rotating the plants is a simple technique to keep the African violets looking superb and the envy of all your friends. They will be forever quizzing you, trying to discover your secret for being so successful.

African violets prefer low light intensities for long periods of time. In the summer, when there is twelve to sixteen hours of daylight they do very well on windowsills, provided the plants aren't placed in direct sunlight. However, most African violets are tucked away somewhere in the house where the natural lighting is inadquate. The light filters through the windows, barely reaching the plants, keeping them alive. Occasionally they will flower under these conditions. The addition of supplemental lighting will greatly enhance the appearance of plants in the remote, dark corners of your home.

Using artificial lighting will allow you to grow African violets anywhere you desire, provided the plants' other cultural needs are also met. Places such as bookshelves, room dividers, basements, under cabinets, or just about any other spot you wish to try will make excellent locations for African violets to grow under lights.

When looking for a spot for your plants consider the temperature around the immediate area, the air movement, and how convenient and accessible the plants will be. You want to get to them easily to tend to their needs and to show them off to your friends.

Light Requirements of African Violets

The beauty of an African violet can be measured by the amount of light it receives. Too little light, and the plants will refuse to flower. However, the leaves of the plants are really the best indicator of whether or not they are receiving proper lighting. Spindly leaves reaching toward the ceiling show a plant that is not receiving enough light. Dark-green leaves hanging over the edge of the pot, heading toward the tabletop, are receiving too much light. They look as if they are trying to get away from the light by hiding under the pot. Perfect lighting is indicated by leaves which are practically parallel to the tabletop, with just a few leaves in the center of the rosette peeking up at the light.

The key to having healthy flowering African violets is getting the proper balance between the length of time the light shines on the plants and having the light intensities at the best possible level. General Electric Company Division at Cleveland, Ohio, has done extensive research in the area of using artificial lights for growing African violets. The results of some of this work is shown in the table below which illustrates how the amount of light affects the beauty of African violets.

		Length of time plants were exposed to 600 footcandles of light.		
		6 Hrs.	12 Hrs.	18 Hrs.
African violets	leaves	45	54	56
response to the	flower stalks	19	23	28
light	flowers	92	181	239

160

The purpose of using artificial lights is to improve the attractiveness of your African violets. Proper manipulation of the number of hours of light your plants receive can have a tremendous effect on their flowering. This means that the number of flowers produced by a plant can be used as a measuring stick of your success at growing African violets under artificial light conditions.

Twelve to fourteen hours of light a day is sufficient for African violets. It is important that the light is continuous and not interrupted with any periods of total darkness. The total number of flowers is greatly influenced by the length of the lighted period. Look back at the last table and you can easily see that the plants produced twice as many flowers when given twelve hours of light as compared to just six hours. It is not uncommon for some African violets to produce over two hundred blossoms per plant when grown under proper lighting.

African violets should never receive more than sixteen hours of light in any twenty four hours. Continuous overexposure to light will cause the plants to become unhealthy and malformed. The best way to insure that lights are ''on'' and ''off'' at the correct time is to use a timing switch.

Brightness of the light plays an important part in the flowering of African violets. If you leave the light on for twelve to fourteen hours but it is too dim the plants won't reach their full flowering potential. As little as 50 to 100 footcandles of light is sufficient for plant growth, but it will hardly do for producing those lovely blossoms you are seeking. African violets require 400 to 650 footcandles for average growth requirements and will produce flowers for you at these light intensities. If you really want your plants to become prolific bloomers give them 800 to 1,000 footcandles of light for twelve hours every day of the week. You'll be absolutely astounded at the results.

BRIGHTNESS OF THE LIGHT IN FOOT CANDLES

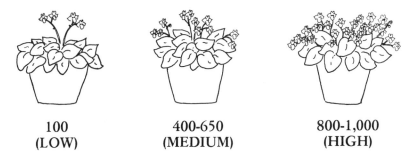

| 100 | 400-650 | 800-1,000 |
| (LOW) | (MEDIUM) | (HIGH) |

Light plays a key role in an African violet's ability to display its lovely blossoms. As the light shining on the plants becomes brighter, there is an increase in the number of blossoms.

161

Your African violets will be the biggest, most beautiful plants in town.

You will also have to get to know your plants and learn the individual light requirements of each. Some varieties of African violets like a bright light; others do best in filtered, soft light. A few general rules on light requirements of the different types of African violets can be given. Those

Proper placement of your African violets under the lights plays a key role in your becoming a successful indoor gardener. The guide below will help you achieve your goal of growing exquisite African violets.

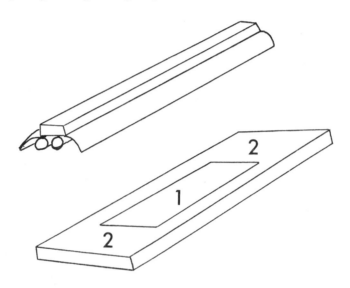

AREA 1 Directly under the Lights

    Place the plants with:
       —dark green foliage
       —blue and purple blossoms
       —double petalled blossoms
       —boy-type foliage
       —young seedlings

AREA 2 Around the Outer Edges of the Light

    Place the plants with:
       —light green foliage
       —pink and white blossoms
       —variegated leaf varieties
       —girl-type foliage

NOTE: When mature, the seedling plants should be moved to the proper location under the lights.

plants with dark-green foliage, blue and purple flowers, and double flowers will need more light than those with light-green leaves and pink and white flowers. Girl-type plants can get by on less light than boy-type African violets. Also, young seedling plants require more light than mature plants. This light sensitivity by the different African violets will determine their position under the lights on a bench setup.

Place the dark-green plants and those with the darker flowers directly under the lights. The light-green leafed African violets, variegated leaf varieties, and plants with pink or white flowers should be placed at the edges of the lighted areas. The brightness of the light is less along the edges than it is directly underneath the lights. The placement of plants under the lights will be discussed again when we look at how to set your lights up over a bench or countertop.

Type of Light Fixtures

Balanced lighting is important if you want your plants to have numerous flowers adorning them. The plants can get by on either incandescent or fluorescent light for a long time, but they will do best when exposed to light from each fixture. The length of time flowers remain on the African violets for you to enjoy is influenced by the type lighting you chose. With balanced lighting you can expect each blossom to last two-and-one-half to three weeks.

Agriculture lamps produce a wide range of light rays which are very suitable for growing African violets. Using these specially developed lamps as the only source of light will encourage plants to develop rapidly and produce numerous blossoms for your enjoyment.

If you want spectacular results, add an incandescent bulb in your lighting setup with the agriculture lamps. It will take several weeks, sixteen to twenty, but once the change manifests itself it will be worth the waiting. The overall appearance of the African violets foliage will have improved, but a tremendous increase in blossoms will be your real reward. You must be patient, for it does take a long time for plants to respond to any subtle changes in light quality.

Light Setup for African Violets

Once you have made up your mind to grow African violets under lights you need to formulate a plan on how to set up an area for this project. First, go out and purchase the necessary supplies; lights, reflectors, and timing switch. Using a manual ''on-off'' switch is okay if you can always be home at the correct time every day. It's best to avoid this situation by investing in

163

African violets can thrive indoors out of the reach of natural sunlight. Fluorescent and agricultural lights duplicate the sunlight and promote healthy, flowering plants by creating ideal growing conditions. *Courtesy of Duro-Lite Lamps, Inc.*

an inexpensive twenty-four hour timing switch. You can set the timer to the amount of light you want the plants to have, and go off to work or the store without having to worry about getting home to turn on the lights.

The longer the fluorescent tube, the more efficient it is. For this reason the forty-eight-inch-long tubes are best whenever it is possible to use them.

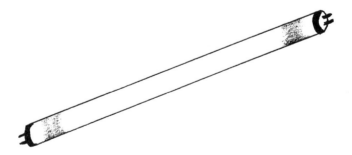

Gray smoke rings at each end of a flourescent tube is an indication it has been in use for many hours. Replace the tube when these rings first appear.

164

These fluorescent fixtures are most frequently rated at 40 watts and are readily available at most stores. Tubes should be replaced once a year or whenever you see gray smoke rings occurring at the ends of the tubes.

A simple setup for your lights would be to use two four-foot fluorescent tubes suspended above the African violets. If you elect to add the light from an incandescent bulb, use the following rule to obtain the proper balance of light. For each watt of incandescent light there should be three watts of fluorescent light. So if you have two 40-watt fluorescent tubes you would need 30 watts of incandescent light. It is better to have a few extra watts of incandescent light than to have too little.

Tired of depending on the sunlight to come out from behind the clouds so that your African violets will receive the light they need to produce those gorgeous blossoms? Below is a simple set-up for building your own plant center in the basement of your home. Growing African violets under lights will cause them to become outstanding bloomers, allowing them to flower year round for your enjoyment. *Courtesy of Sylvania.*

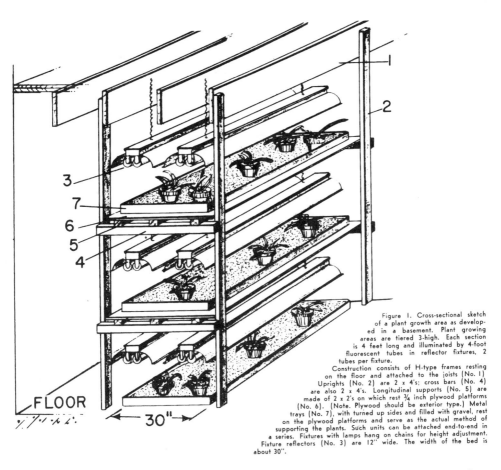

FLOOR

← 30" →

Figure I. Cross-sectional sketch of a plant growth area as developed in a basement. Plant growing areas are tiered 3-high. Each section is 4 feet long and illuminated by 4-foot fluorescent tubes in reflector fixtures, 2 tubes per fixture.

Construction consists of H-type frames resting on the floor and attached to the joists (No. I) Uprights (No. 2) are 2 x 4's; cross bars (No. 4) are also 2 x 4's. Longitudinal supports (No. 5) are made of 2 x 2's on which rest ¾ inch plywood platforms (No. 6). (Note. Plywood should be exterior type.) Metal trays (No. 7), with turned up sides and filled with gravel, rest on the plywood platforms and serve as the actual method of supporting the plants. Such units can be attached end-to-end in a series. Fixtures with lamps hang on chains for height adjustment. Fixture reflectors (No. 3) are 12" wide. The width of the bed is about 30".

165

A common practice followed by many artificial light gardeners is to use a 40-watt fluorescent tube in combination with a single agriculture lamp. This gives the plants the various light rays needed for ideal growth and flowering without the need for adding the incandescent lighting.

When trying to determine the size of plant bench or countertop and how many lights to use, follow this simple rule: for each 20 watts of light, plan on one square foot of area under the lights. A single 40-watt fluorescent light would emit enough light for two square feet of bench area. The standard two-lamp fixture (40 watts each) would allow you to grow African violets on a 1 ft. x 4 ft. or a 2 ft. x 2 ft. bench.

Suspend the lights eighteen inches above the countertop where the plants are to be grown. The distance between the lights and the plants will vary, depending on whether the plants are mature or young developing plants.

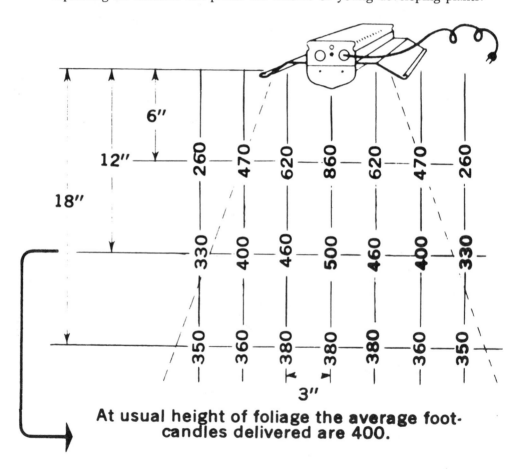

At usual height of foliage the average foot-candles delivered are 400.

Approximate foot-candle values on plants 6 to 18 inches from two 40-watt Cool White fluorescent fixtures. *Courtesy of General Electric.*

The younger the plants, the closer they should be moved to the lights. If you are using the agriculture lamps the leaves of the plants should be twelve to fourteen inches below the lights. The fluorescent lights give off a small amount of heat, so do not have the lights so low that the plant leaves actually touch the tubes. The lights should never be any closer to plants than four inches.

One final point needs to be made about lighting setups and how the brightness of light varies under the fluorescent tubes. The last illustration points out the variation of the light's brightness as it spreads out over a bench area. You can easily see why the plants that like bright light should be directly under the lights and not along the edges.

Propagation Under Lights

A complete chapter was devoted to propagation of African violets and the techniques to use to be successful. Now, you may wish to try your luck in starting new plants under artificial lights. The results will really amaze you.

From the time of taking a leaf cutting to when the new plant will begin flowering is a short four months. Usually under natural sunlight five to eight months or longer must pass before you see the first flowers. Plants started from seed under lights will flower for you in six to nine months. When dividing bigger African violets it's just a matter of a few weeks until the plants get over the shock of your treating them so roughly. Once they recover they'll start flowering immediately for you again.

Care of African Violets

African violets grown under lights require about the same care as those grown in natural sunlight. The important difference to remember, however, is when you place plants under lights you are giving them an ideal growing condition for twelve to fourteen hours a day.

Three factors in your care of growing African violets under lights must be adjusted to meet the increased demands of the plants as they are rapidly growing and flowering. These factors are: water, fertilizing and temperature. Proper balancing of each of these is important to the well-being of your African violets.

Due to the longer light periods each day the plants' growth will increase. This means they will be using more water. You need to schedule your watering to insure that the plants never dry out, otherwise beautiful African violets can wilt and die very quickly when grown under lights.

There is little need to worry about getting small amounts of water on the leaves of the plants when they are growing under lights. The light from the fluorescent tubes will not burn the leaves unless you allow the plants to grow too close to the fixtures. However, it is always a good practice not to get water on the leaves whenever possible.

You still have to avoid getting the crowns of the plants wet. The disease, crown rot, is just as much of a threat to African violets whether grown under artificial lights or in natural light.

When an African violet is grown under artificial lighting it is being given the ideal light for the best growing conditions. In order to take advantage of this it is important to keep the plants well fed. Plants growing twelve to fourteen hours a day have a tremendous appetite. To meet the plants' needs you should fertilize at least once every two weeks. An adequate supply of food will help to insure they become as big and beautiful as you anticipate.

Temperature requirements of African violets growing under the lights aren't much different from temperatures which are favorable for healthy growth in sunlight. Maintain the temperature between 65 to 75 degrees F. and your plants will be happy. Avoid locating the plants anywhere they may be exposed to sudden changes in temperature. For example, don't place them near an outside door where a blast of cold air comes in every time the door is opened.

Spacing of Plants

African violets should not be crowded together under the lights. They need plenty of room for their rosette of leaves to grow out over the edge of the pot. The plants are too close together if the leaves from different plants touch each other. Air movement and the humidity around the plants is interfered with when the plants are placed too close together.

Disease organisms and insect pests can easily spread from one plant to another if plants are crowded up under the lights. Leave ample room for your African violets to develop and so you can easily work among the plants without disturbing them.

Back to Natural Light

Many gardeners who produce healthy flowering African violets under artificial lighting have found that when these plants are moved back into natural light they blossom less and lose some of their vigor.

This is easily explained. Under artificial lights the plants have been given ideal growing conditions with optimum lighting, causing them to be gorgeous. When moved to another area of the house, where they have to depend on natural light for shorter periods of time, plants go into a mild stage of shock. You've taken them from their plush, cozy home and set them down in a new environment. But given time, the African violets will adapt to these new conditions and once again produce those beautiful purple, pink, red and white blossoms for your enjoyment.

13
A Special African Violet Shopping Guide

In the following pages you will find a wealth of information on where to buy African violets, special products developed for use with these plants and descriptions of over 135 individual varieties.

In this chapter it is my goal to give every African violet enthusiast the opportunity to select and to obtain new plants with the exciting features very seldom seen in plants sold in most garden centers and florist shops. The variety displayed by these marvelous indoor favorites has caused many homes to become havens for African violets by the hundreds.

The demand for these popular indoor flowering plants is absolutely astounding! Plant mania has created such a clamor for African violets that the commercial growers are having a difficult time supplying enough plants. To give you an example, consider the grower who produces over 200,000 plants every year—and could sell more, but limited space and help prevents it.

Several hobbyists who started out with only a few African violets, soon found themselves adding another room or even a greenhouse to their home to accommodate all their plants. After numerous expansions, these expert growers started selling their lovely plants, first to local stores and then branched out to service customers in the United States, Canada, England, and throughout the world.

African Violet Specialty Stores

Interest in growing African violets has been increasing tremendously as more and more gardening enthusiasts have discovered the beauty of these

170

magnificent plants. Most of the plants available to hobbyists at their local garden centers are plain leaf varieties with red, white, or purple blossoms. The newer, more exciting African violets can be enjoyed by everyone who is fascinated by this plant. African violets with variegated foliage, ruffled or fluted leaf margins, semidouble or double blossoms, miniature plants, frilled blossoms—are just a few of the beautiful characteristics that can be discovered by acquiring the latest hybrids which have been developed by growers throughout the world.

To give every African violet hobbyist the opportunity of displaying the newest hybrids in their homes, a representative list was compiled of speciality stores, greenhouses, nurseries, and private growers. Besides the latest in African violet varieties, these suppliers also have specialty items for growing these delicate plants. The following is only a partial list of growers who are dedicated to the promotion of the world's most popular flowering houseplant. A quick check around where you live may turn up an African violet speciality store close enough for you to personally visit and select your plants.

A special code has been prepared showing the services and specialty products available from each supplier. Compare the numbers found after each of the addresses with the code, and you'll find your decision on who to contact will be much easier.

Code of Services Available from Suppliers

1. African violet plants.
2. Cuttings (leaves).
3. Seeds.
4. Plant food.
5. Pots and other containers.
6. Special African violet soil mixtures.
7. Artificial lighting setups.
8. Insecticides.
9. Gardening books on African violets.
10. Ship cuttings (leaves).
11. Ship plants.
12. Open to visitors.
13. Visitors by appointment only.
14. Catalog available on request.

United States

Annalee Violetry
29-50   214th Place
Bayside, New York 11360
Phone: 212-224-3376

Services: 1,2,7,9,10,11,13,14 (send 25 cents for a catalog)

Wilson Brothers Floral Company, Inc.
Roachdale, Indiana 46172
Phone: 317-596-3455

Services: 1,2,3,4,5,6,7,8,9,10,11,12,14

Utopia Greenhouses
P.O. Box 313 US 64
Hayesville, N.C. 28904
Phone: 704-389-6708

Services: 1,4,5,6,8,9,11,12,14

Fischer Greenhouses
Oak Avenue
Linwood, New Jersey 08221
Phone: 609-927-3399

Services: 1,2,4,5,6,7,8,9,11,12,14
          (cuttings only shipped overseas)

Baker's African Violets
P.O. Box 1106
Tucker, Georgia 30084
Phone: 404-934-7827

Services: 1,14 (send 25 cents for catalog)

Tomara African Violets
Rt. No. 3
Fayette, Missouri 65248
Phone: 816-248-3232

Services: 1,2,7,10,11,12,14 (send 25 cents for catalog)

St. Louis Violet Nurseries
48 Queensbrook
St. Louis, Missouri 63132
Phone: 314-997-6831

Services: 3,14 (send 25 cents for catalog)

Violet Fantasia
15414 Heimer Road
San Antonio, Texas 78232
Phone: 512-494-7829

Services: 1,2,10,11,14 (send 25 cents for catalog)

The Green House
9515 Flower Street
Bellflower, California 90706
Phone: 213-925-0870

Services: 1,4,5,6,7,8,9,12,14

Klinkel's African Violets
1553 Harding Street
Enumclaw, Washington 98022
Phone: 206-825-4442

Services: 1,2,4,10,11,13,14 (send 25 cents for catalog)

Tinari Greenhouses
2325 Valley Road
Box 190
Huntingdon Valley, Pennsylvania 19006
Phone: 215-947-0144

Services: 1,4,5,7,8,9,11,12,14 (send 25 cents for catalog)

The Parson's African Violets
3917 Island Home Pike
Knoxville, Tennessee 37920
Phone: 615-573-2236

Services: 1,2,13

DoDe's Gardens
1490 Saturn Street
Merritt Island, Florida 32952

Services: 1,2,4,5,6,7,8,9,10,11,13,14

Dates Violetry
RR. No. 1   Box 72D
Sugar Grove, Illinois 60554
Phone: 312-557-2265

Services: 1,2,10,13,14

Kat's African Violets
40600 Chapel Way No. 3
Fremont, California 94538
Phone: 415-796-1200

Services: 1,2,5,6,13

Violets Atlanta
2581 Piedmont Road
Broadview Plaza
Atlanta, Georgia 30324
Phone: 404-231-0645

Services: 1,4,5,6,7,8,9,10,11,12,14

Lyndon Lyon Greenhouses
14 Mutchler Street
Dolgeville, New York 13329
Phone: 315-429-8291

Services: 1,2,4,5,6,8,10,11,12,14

Reva's Violet Room
92152 Coburg Road
Eugene, Oregon 97401
Phone: 503-484-9974

Services: 1,4,5,6,8,13

174

The Violet Depot
100 Tuscarawas Road
Beaver, Pennsylvania 15009
Phone: 412-774-5208

Services: 1,2,4,5,7,8,10,11,12,14 (send 25 cents for catalog)

Crestwood Violetry
7314 Jervis Street
Springfield, Virginia 22151
Phone: 703-256-1575

Services: 1,2,4,5,6,10,11,13,14 (send 25 cents for catalog)

Steve & Sue's Bear Valley Garden Center
3651 South Sheridan
Denver, Colorado 80235
Phone: 303-988-2441

Services: 1,2,4,5,6,8,9,11,12

Bonneville Nursery
1118W 450N
Provo, Utah 84601
Phone: 801-375-7013

Services: 1,2,13

Canada

Wood's African Violets
Proton Station,
Ontario NOC 1LO
Phone: 519-923-3409

Services: 1,2,4,5,6,7,8,9,10,12,14 (send 30 cents for catalog)

The Plant Place
P.O. Box 936
New Hamburg,
Ontario NOB 2GO
Phone: 519-662-2473

Services: 1,2,4,5,6,10,11,13,14 (send 75 cents for catalog; refunded with initial order)

Phipps African Violets
RR NO. 1
Paris,
Ontario N3L 3E1
Phone: 519-442-2870

Services: 1,2,4,5,6,7,8,9,10,11,12,14 (send 25 cents for catalog)

Sanmar's Violetry
70 Enfield Avenue
Toronto,
Ontario M8W 1T9
Phone: 416-251-6369

Services: 1,2,7,10,12,14 (send 50 cents for catalog)

Simpson's African Violets
6715 Randolph Avenue
Burnaby,
British Columbia V5H 3W3
Phone: 604-433-6757

Services: 1,2,10,11,13,14

The Scott's
P.O. Box 346
Lachine,
Quebec H8S 4C2
Phone: 514-484-8961

Services: 1,2,4,5,6,7,8,9,10,11,12,14

Australia

Kenrose & Company
1 Yarrabin Road
Kenthurst 2154
N.S.W. Australia
Phone: 02-654-1016

Services: 1,4,5,6,7,12

176

Hong Kong

Cecilia Florist
B2 Bagnio Villa
550 Victoria Road
Phone: 5-510 708

Services: 1,4,5,6,8,12

England

The major growers of African violets listed here supply florist shops, garden centers, and stores with beautiful plants from their greenhouses. African violet enthusiasts may arrange for guided tours to obtain firsthand knowledge of how these plants are commercially grown. Arrangements must be made in advance with the growers.

It would not be unusual for a single grower to have as many as 250,000 African violets under one greenhouse roof. One grower told of producing over 750,000 plants a year for sale in England. Fresh plants are selected daily and removed from the greenhouses for delivery to customers.

Rochfords Houseplants
Turnford Hall Nurseries
Turnford, Broxbourne,
Hertfordshire EN10 6BH
Phone: Hoddesdon 64512

Lynn Houseplants Ltd.
African Violet Nurseries
Station Road
Terrington St. Clements
King's Lynn
Norfolk PE34 4PL
Phone: King's Lynn 828374

Northmoor Nurseries
Northmoor, Oxford

Leeslane Nurseries
Dalton, Parbold
Wigan, Lancashire

Thomas Butcher Ltd.
Shirley, East Croydon,
Surrey

Plants Received Through the Mail

When ordering African violets from specialty stores there are a few guidelines which you should be aware of to expedite shipment of your plants.

Before ordering any plants, write and request a catalog or a listing of available plants. Usually, along with the catalog or listing of plants, you will receive other information needed to place an order.

First, notice when the store will ship plants to you. April 1st to May 1st is about as early in the year as you can expect a store to mail your order. Any sooner, and there is an excellent chance of cold weather damage to the plants. Some stores will ship in the winter months but only at the buyer's risk. October 31st is the cut-off date established for shipping plants.

Usually there is a minimum order. However, this doesn't present a problem since there are so many beautiful new varieties from which to choose. Remittance along with the order is a standard request and insures quick handling of your order.

Foreign orders should always be placed well in advance. This will allow time for your order to be received, and it also gives the grower the necessary time needed to prepare your plant material for shipping. Check with the suitable government offices to determine what steps must be taken to allow plant materials to be shipped into the country. Often all you will need is to furnish an import permit with your order. Payment on any foreign order is usually made by bank drafts.

Plants Need Attention When Received

Plants shipped through the mail or by United Parcel will usually arrive in good condition. Sometimes, if the package was delayed in route, plant leaves will be wilting. Don't panic! With proper treatment, and a few days of tender loving care, these plants will return to their normal appearance for you to enjoy.

Give the plants a drink of water right away and watch the leaves perk up. Be careful not to overwater the plants during the first week to ten days after you receive them. Allowing the new plants to adapt to their new home is important to their overall vigor in the months to come.

178

Place your new African violets in a bright, sunny location, but avoid putting them in any direct sunlight. You can place the new plants under artificial lights right away without having to worry about any damage being done to them.

Don't forget to isolate the new plants from the rest of your African violets. You may wish to consider treating them with an insecticide once or twice to further assure yourself that your new plants aren't harboring any mites, aphids, mealybugs, white flies, or any other insect pests.

African Violet Shopping List

Tired of growing the same old African violets that everyone else has sitting on their windowsills? Are you ready to add some of the newer, more fascinating plants available from African violet specialty stores to your collection?

If your answer was ''yes'' to both of these questions, then look over the following list of African violets and choose plants with the unique features you want displayed in your home for your enjoyment. After completing your selection, thumb through the previous section on African Violet Specialty Stores, and choose one from which to order your new plants. Most of these stores will mail you a catalog, for a nominal price, with color photographs showing what the individual plant features are.

After Dark	Dark purple, double blossoms. Quilted, ovate foliage. Standard.
Alakazam	Double, fuchsia, star blossoms, some petals purple. Quilted foliage. Standard
Alice's Cochise	Striking red, double flowers. Plain, supreme foliage. Standard.
Ann Slocomb	Double, pink blooms. Wavy, ovate foliage. Large.
Autumn Russet	Rose russet, fringed, double blossoms. Quilted, ruffled foliage. Standard.
Bali Hai	Semidouble, pink flowers with ruffled edges. Dark-green, ovate, quilted foliage. Standard.
Ballet Anna	Single, wavy, shell-pink blooms. Plain foliage. Standard.
Ballet Lisa	Frilled, glowing-pink, single flowers. Plain foliage. Standard.
Becky	Enormous peachy-pink, semidouble flowers. Wavy, red-backed, tapered foliage. Standard.
Blizzard	Striking white, double, star blossoms; sometimes marked with pink. Tailored shiny foliage. Standard.

179

Bloomin' Fool	Medium blue, double flowers. Dark ovate foliage. Standard.
Blue Boy	Dark violet, single blossoms. Ovate pointed foliage. Standard.
Blue Reverie	Semidouble, light-blue blossoms with lighter blue fringe. Quilted, wavy foliage. Standard.
Blue Storm	Purplish blue, double, star blossoms. Plain, variegated foliage. Standard.
Brigadoon	Semidouble, bright-red blossoms with white edges. Plain, quilted, pointed foliage. Standard.
Bullseye	Huge, single, fuchsia-pink, star blossoms with white edges. Quilted, tailored foliage. Standard.
Butterfly White	Semidouble, snow-white, star blossoms. Plain, ovate foliage. Standard.
Candy Lips	Double, white blossoms with red edges. Ovate foliage. Standard.
Champion's Water Lily	Double, light-pink blossoms. Quilted, wavy, variegated foliage. Standard.
Chanticleer	Double, light-pink flowers. Dark, quilted, ovate and pointed foliage. Standard.
Charmglow	Blossoms light rose-lavender, fringed, semi-doubles with maroon two-tone tipping. Plain, quilted foliage. Large.
Christi Love	Double, coral flowers. Nearly black red-backed foliage. Standard.
Clipper	Double, white, star flowers. Plain, pointed foliage. Standard.
Copper Tips	Dark ivory, two-toned, double blossoms; tipped in rose-copper colors. Tailored foliage. Standard.
Coral Caper	Double, reddish-violet, star-shaped flowers. Plain foliage. Standard.
Coral Cascade	Single, reddish-pink bloom with darker center. Plain foliage. Standard.
Coral Reef	Double, deep coral flowers, edged in white. Plain, pointed foliage. Standard.
Cordelia	Double, pink, star blooms with darker tips. Plain, variegated leaves. Standard.
Cousin Janet	Deep purplish-blue, double, star blossoms with white edges. Round, pointed leaves. Small standard.
Crimson Frost	Double, fringed, red blooms with white edges. Young plants heavily variegated, some mature plants may not show variegation. Standard.
Crown of Red	Floriferous, double, red blossoms. Smooth, ovate, slightly wavy leaves. Standard.
Dancing Doll	Bright pink, double, star blossoms. Ovate foliage.

180

	Semiminiature.
Dazzling Deceiver	Double, rose-pink flowers. Plain, glossy foliage. Standard.
Delft Imperial	Blue, two-toned, fringed, double blossoms. Sometimes has petals with white edges. Quilted, scalloped, and pointed leaves. Standard.
Dora Baker	Double, pink blooms. Quilted, ovate foliage. Compact grower. Semiminiature.
Double Black Cherry	Wine-red, double flowers. Large quilted leaves. Standard.
Duet	Bright blue, double blossoms with white edges. Dark tailored foliage. Standard.
Edith V. Peterson	Flowers double, two-toned orchid, stars with deeper edging. Plain foliage. Large.
Emperor	Double, pale-pink blossoms with upper half of petals tipped with red. Very dark ovate foliage. Large.
Faith	Double, fringed, pure-white blooms. Quilted, ovate and pointed foliage. Standard.
Firebird	Fringed, single flowers with red centers and a broad white border. Wavy foliage. Small standard.
Flamingo	Double, ruffled, deep rosy-pink flowers. Plain foliage. Standard.
Floral Fantasy	Double, mauve, star blossoms with splashes of wisteria blue. Plain foliage. Standard.
Frankie	Semidouble, dark royal-blue, star blossoms. Plain, slightly serrated foliage. Standard.
Garnet Elf	Fringed, dark rose-lavender, single blooms; broad white border. Ruffled foliage. Standard.
Gotcha	Fuschia, double, ruffled, star blossoms; often appears single. Quilted, ovate foliage. Standard.
Granger's Blue Fashionaire	Double, medium blue blooms. Plain, pointed foliage. Standard.
Granger's Carefree	Double, light blue-lavender blossoms with white edges. Plain, quilted foliage. Standard.
Granger's Fashionaire	Double, fluted, lavender-pink, two-toned blooms. Plain, quilted foliage. Large.
Granger's Festival	Double, white, fringed, star blossoms with red edges. Ruffled, variegated foliage. Standard.
Granger's Garden's Snow Ballet	Camellia-type white, double blossoms. Pointed, quilted foliage. Standard.
Granger's Peach Frost	Full double, ivory-peach flowers, upper petals copper-tipped. Plain, quilted, pointed foliage. Large.
Granger's Peppermint	Double, fringed, white flowers with red edging.

Quilted, ruffled, variegated foliage. Large.

Granger's Pied Piper	Double, blue-white blooms. plain, quilted and pointed foliage. Standard.
Granger's Serenity	Double, fringed, white flowers; dark purple, ruffled edges. Ruffled foliage. Standard.
Happy Harold	Single blossoms, red to wine colored. Plain, variegated foliage. Standard.
Happy Time	Double, rose-pink, star blossoms. Slightly quilted foliage. Standard.
Helene	Deep fuchsia-red, semidouble flowers. Dark foliage. Standard.
Hello Dolly	Double, medium-pink, star blossoms. Ovate, medium-strawberry foliage. Standard.
Henny Backus	Double, purple, star blossoms. Plain, glossy foliage. Standard.
Ivy Peach	Double, light-peach, star blossoms with darker petal tips. Smooth, ovate foliage. Standard.
Janny	Single flowers, star-shaped, lavender-pink with white edges. Medium-green foliage. Standard.
Jason	Double, light purplish-red, fringed blossoms. Medium-green, plain foliage with serrated edge. Standard.
Jennifer	Single, lightly cupped, pale lavender blooms, border of dark lavender and narrow white to green edge. Longifolia, pointed foliage. Standard.
Jingle Bells	Brilliant raspberry-rose, frilled, double blossoms. Slightly rippled foliage. Standard.
Jolly Giant	Frosty-pink, semidouble blossoms. Flat, serrated foliage. Standard.
Kathleen	Pure-white, double blossoms. Round, smooth foliage. Standard.
Lavender Delight	Double, light lavender, star blossoms with dark lavender flecks. Plain, medium-green foliage. Standard.
Lavender Tempest	Double, fringed, lavender-pink blossoms with red petal tipping. Plain, quilted and pointed foliage. Standard.
Like Wow	Semidouble, royal purple, star blossoms; sometimes has white edges. Occasionally appears as a single blossom. Plain foliage, Standard.
Lillian Jarrett	Light-pink, double flowers. Pointed, quilted, serrated leaves. Large.
Lullaby	Flowers light blue, doubles with lighter blue, almost white, shading. Plain, quilted foliage. Standard.

Mary C	Semidouble, clear pink, star blossoms. Quilted, slightly ovate foliage. Standard.
Mary D	Double, dark-red, star blossoms. Plain, tailored foliage. Standard.
Magnifica	Double, fuchsia, star blossoms with white edges. Smooth, round leaves. Standard.
Master Blue	Bluish-purple blooms with white edges. Double, star-shaped blossoms. Plain ovate foliage. Standard.
Midget Bon Bon	Single, pink blooms with darker center. Plain variegated foliage. Miniature.
Miriam Steel	Double, fringed, white, star blossoms. Sometimes has some pink in the petals. Plain foliage. Standard.
Mrs. Greg	Double, lavender, star flowers. Plain, pointed foliage. Standard.
My Darling	Double, cherry-pink blooms. Quilted, ovate, cupped up foliage. Large.
Nancy Reagan	Double, dark red-wine blooms; darker red on tips. Plain, variegated foliage. Standard to large.
Nona Weber	Semidouble, star blossoms. Red orchid, rayed from light center to purple edge to lavender edge. Plain, slightly quilted and pointed foliage. Standard.
Orion	Double, white blooms. Plain foliage. Standard.
Peak Of Pink	Full open pink-and-white, semidouble, star blossoms. Ovate, quilted foliage. Standard.
Pink Jester	Medium pink, full double blossoms. Medium-green, plain, quilted, pointed foliage. Standard.
Pink Panther	Blossoms rose-pink to rose, double, stars. Ovate foliage. Standard.
Pink Viceroy	Double, deep-pink blooms. Plain, pointed foliage. Standard.
Pixie Blue	Single, purplish-blue flowers with slightly deeper-colored centers. Plain, ovate foliage. Miniature trailer.
Pixie Trail	Small violet-shaped, pink flowers with deeper centers. Plain leaves. Semiminiature trailer.
Plain and Fancy	Double blossoms, ruffled, pink, stars. Plain, quilted, variegated foliage. Large.
Plum Tip	Light lavender, star, single blossoms; deep plum red tips. Quilted, plain leaves. Standard.
Pocono Mountains	Flowers semidouble, purple, geneva, stars with darker purple edges. Tailored foliage. Standard.
Poodle Top	Fringed, double blossoms with lavender-pink to rose-lavender petals which show a faint tinge of

	green occasionally. Plain, slightly pointed foliage. Standard.
Prom Queen	Single blossoms, medium blue with white margins on fluted petals. Medium olive-green, tailored foliage. Standard.
Purple Choice	Double blossoms with white edges. Tailored foliage. Standard.
Radiation	Single, pink blossoms with reddish-pink eye radiating toward the edges. Ruffled foliage. Standard.
Red Flame	Deep-red, semidouble flowers. Medium-green, tailored foliage. Standard.
Red Honey	Large fuchsia-red, double blossoms. Shiny, tailored, waxy foliage. Standard.
Regina	Double, pure white blooms; occasionally one may have lavender coloring. Plain, quilted, ovate foliage. Standard.
Rhapsodie Claudia	Clear-pink, single flowers. Very large flowers. Plain leaves. Standard.
Rhapsodie Elfriede	Dark-blue, single blossoms. Quilted foliage. Standard.
Rhapsodie Gigi	Semidouble, white flowers with a blue band. Plain, quilted foliage. Standard.
Rhapsodie Gisela	Clear-pink, single blossoms. Small dark-green leaves. Standard.
Rhapsodie Mars	Ruby-red blooms. Tailored foliage. Standard.
Rhapsodie Ophelia	Plum-red, semidouble blossoms, center shaded darker. Plain dark tailored foliage. Standard.
Richter's Step Up	Semidouble, deep-blue blooms. Smooth, ovate foliage. Standard.
Richter's Wedgewood	Double, light-blue flowers. Very dark, fluted foliage. Standard.
Royalaire	Double blossoms, royal blue with white edging. Plain, quilted foliage. Standard.
Ruffled Red	Blossoms semidouble, deep red, stars. Plain, ruffled foliage. Standard.
Sailor's Dream	Fluffy double blossoms, light blue. Dark wavy foliage. Standard.
Seafoam	Single, fringed, medium-blue blooms with broad white edges. Quilted, wavy foliage. Small standard.
Silver Crest	White, ruffled, double blossoms with blue edges. Variegated ovate, ruffled foliage. Standard.
Softique	Pale pink, double flowers. Slightly fluted, ovate, quilted foliage. Standard.
Spring Deb	Double, white-faced blooms with blue ruffled edges. Ruffled foliage. Standard.

184

Starshine	Single, white, star blooms. Plain, pointed foliage. Standard.
Strawberry Shortcake	Large, vivid red-pink, double blossoms. Deep green, plain foliage. Large.
Sweet Mary	Blossoms double, plum-wine, stars with deeper colored veins. Plain, quilted and pointed foliage. Standard.
Sweet Pixie	Double, light-pink blooms. Plain, slightly pointed foliage. Semiminiature.
The King	Double, dark-blue to purple blooms. Plain, tailored foliage. Standard.
The Parson's Wife	Pink-edged and stripped, ruffled, single, white blossoms. Quilted and ruffled foliage. Large.
Tina	Double, garnet-fuchsia blooms. Plain foliage. Standard.
Tinted Frills	Blossoms pink-and-white, frilled, stars. Fluted, variegated foliage. Standard.
Tipt	Lavender, two-toned, single blossoms. Tailored foliage. Standard.
Tommie Lou	White, very light orchid in center, double blossoms. Plain quilted, dark-green, variegated foliage, feathered with white edges. Large.
Top Dollar	Double, dark-bluish purple blooms. Plain, variegated foliage. Standard.
Triple Threat	Double, bright pink, star blossoms. Scalloped foliage. Standard.
Vern's Delight	Semidouble, royal blue, star flowers with white edges. Plain, quilted, pointed foliage. Standard.
Violet Trail	Between mauve and amethyst, single, star blooms. Plain, glossy foliage. Standard.
Whirlaway	Purplish-blue, double, star blossoms with white edges. Round, plain foliage. Standard.
White Madonna	White, double blossoms. Girl-type foliage. Standard.
White Perfection	Blossoms full double, white, stars. Plain leaves. Standard.
White Pride	White, double flowers. Plain leaves. Large.
Wild Country	Blue violet, semidouble flowers. Dark-green foliage. Standard.
Wild Flame	Ruffled, single blossoms, fuchsia with white edges. Plain foliage. Standard.
Window Blue	Double, dark-blue blossoms. Plain, pointed foliage. Miniature.
Wisteria	Double, lavender blooms. Plain, glossy foliage. Large.
Wrangler	Blossoms double, fuchsia, stars. Plain, glossy

	foliage. Standard.
Zephyr	Pure white, double blossoms, slightly ruffled.
	Foliage plain. Standard.

The African violet hybrids listed here were selected from the Master List of African violets with the permission of the African Violet Society of America. This is only a partial list of the thousands of hybrids available. The complete list of African violets, along with their descriptions, is available by writing to the address below and requesting a copy of the Master List.

African Violet Society of America
P.O. Box 1326
Knoxville, Tennessee 37901

Glossary of African Violet Terminology

Acid Soil:	Any soil that has a pH of less than 7.
Agricultural lamps:	Special fluorescent light fixtures that emit a high percent of light in the red and blue wavelengths; produce a rose or purplish colored glow when turned on.
Alkaline soil:	Any soil that has a pH greater than 7.
Amazons:	Plants with larger than normal leaves and flowers, usually with thicker leaves. Increased size due to a doubling of the normal chromosome count in all the plant cells.
Angstrom:	A unit of measurement used by scientists for measuring the size of extremely small objects.
Anthers:	Two yellow, saclike structures found on the tip of the stamen in the center of the flower. These saclike structures contain the pollen grains.
Anthocyanin:	Colored pigments found in the cells of the plant, usually red, purple, or varying shades of these two colors.
Artificial lighting:	Light other than that being emitted by the sun. Sources of this type lighting are incandescent bulbs, fluorescent tubes, and agricultural lamps.
Balanced lighing:	Light that is composed of proper ratio of the red and blue wavelengths which causes the plant to be healthy and a profuse bloomer.
Bi-colored blossoms:	Flowers that display two or more colors on each petal.
Blossom:	Synonymous with flower.
Boy-type leaf:	Plain, green leaves, with smooth leaf edges.
Calcine clay:	A processed clay baked at high temperatures to give it better water-holding capacity. Frequently used as a soil additive to improve soil mixtures.
Calyx:	Green, leaf-like floral parts forming a cuplike structure around the base of the flower. Individually each leaf-like structure is called a sepal.
Carotenoid:	A group of colored pigments—yellow, orange, and shades of these colors—found in the cells of plants.

187

Chemical fertilizer:	Any manufactured plant food, usually considered to be easily dissolved by water. Releases the nutrients quickly for plant utilization.
Chlorophyll:	A green pigment found in the cells of all green plants. Essential pigment for photosynthesis to occur in plants.
Chloroplasts:	Small structures found in the sap of cells. Chlorophyll pigment is contained within the chloroplasts.
Chromosome:	Microscopic, rodlike structures composed of individual units (called genes) which pass on the plant's characteristics from generation to generation.
Clone:	Refers to the vegetative propagation of plants by means of cuttings, divisions or separations, so that all new plants will be identical to the original plant.
Compost:	A rich, organic mixture composed of decaying plant parts, fertilizer and soil. Often used to enrich potting soil.
Corolla:	A collective term, referring to all the petals of an individual flower. In African violets the five petals of a single flower or the ten petals of a double flower compose the corolla.
Crossbreeding:	Using the pollen from one African violet and transferring it to the stigma of another plant.
Cross-pollinate:	See crossbreeding.
Crown:	That portion of an African violet plant located just above the soil surface; new leaves and flower stalks originate from the crown.
Cultivars:	Plants that have been developed by plant breeders in their quest for newer African violets.
Cuttings:	A portion of a plant removed for the purpose of growing new plants. In African violets it refers to the removal of individual leaves for starting new plants.
Disbudding:	Removal of flower buds before they have a chance to open.
Division:	Cutting apart the crown of an overgrown African violet; a vegetative means of increasing the number of plants in a collection.
Dominant gene:	Heredity unit on a chromosome that determines which characteristic will be displayed by the plant. Only one gene in a matched pair has to be dominant for the trait to mask the other plant characteristic.
Double blossom:	Flowers that have two sets of petals, one on top of the other. Total number of petals is ten.
DuPont:	See Amazons.
Essential nutrients:	Sixteen different plant foods found in soil and air; all are required by the African violets for healthy growth

188

	and flowering.
Fantasy blossoms:	Blossoms that have streaks or blotches of color on the petals, as if sprinkled with paint; these markings may be a deeper shade of the color of petals or an entirely different color.
Fertilizer:	Any material containing plant food; may be applied to soil in liquid or granular form or sprayed on leaves. Most often contains nitrogen, phosphorus, and potassium.
Fertilizer salts:	Individual plant nutrients that, when dissolved in water and misapplied, can burn a plant's foliage or roots.
Fertilizer solution:	Plant food dissolved in water.
Fluorescent lights:	A type of light fixture especially well suited for use in artificial lighting setups. Several different types are available; cool-white, warm-white, and daylight are the three commonly used.
Foot candles:	A term used to measure the brightness of the light reaching the plants. Scientifically, it is defined as the amount of light one candle radiates on an object one foot from the flame.
Gametes:	The plant structures that carry the hereditary units (genes) for sexual reproduction in plants. The male gamete is the pollen, and the female gamete the unfertilized egg or ovule.
Garden loam:	A garden soil usually rich in organic matter and dark in color.
Gene:	The smallest hereditary unit which passes characteristics from one generation to the next; located on the chromosomes.
Geneva variety:	Plants which have white edges around the flower petals.
Germ tube:	A tubular growth from pollen grain that grows down through the style into the ovary of the flower. Transmittal of chromosomes from pollen to ovary is through the germ tube.
Girl-type leaf:	Leaves with pale-green to white splotches at the base of the leaf where the petiole is attached. Leaves will also have scalloped edges.
Grade (of a fertilizer):	The percent of nitrogen, phosphorus, and potassium contained in a fertilizer.
Hard water:	Culinary water which contains a large amount of soluble salts (iron, calcium, magnesium).
Humus:	Partically decomposed organic materials found in the soil. Adds nutrients, improves soil, retains moisture and provides a better environment for the growth of plant roots.

189

Hybrid:	A plant developed from cross-pollinating two plants that are different, producing offspring with new characteristics.
Hybridization:	See crossbreeding.
Incandescent lights:	First light bulbs developed; produce a high amount of red light rays that promote flowering in plants.
Indifferent plants:	Flowering plants that will produce flowers regardless of the length of daylight. African violets belong to this group.
Kerb cycle:	A complicated series of chemical reactions that occur in the roots of a plant; the end result of this process is the formation of chemical energy used for the plants growth.
Leach:	The movement of water down through the soil, dissolving plant food and removing it as it passes through.
Liebig's theory:	In the late 1700s a German scientist demonstrated a plant's ability to use carbon and oxygen from the air and the individual plant nutrients from the soil. This became known as Liebig's theory until accepted years later by scientists.
Light intensity:	Refers to the brightness of the light, artificial or natural, that shines on the plants.
Light meter:	Small mechanical device used to measure the light intensities (brightness); registers readings in foot candles.
Lighting setup:	Arrangement of lights over a bench, countertop, or any other location where plants are being grown under artificial light conditions.
Lime:	Chemical substance composed of calcium and magnesium that is added to the soil to change the pH of an acid soil.
Long-day plants:	Plants that produce flowers only when there are fourteen to sixteen hours of light shining on them each day.
Macronutrients:	The six major plant-food elements (nitrogen, phosphorus, potassium, sulfur, calcium, and magnesium) needed in large quantities by plants for normal growth and development.
Major nutrients:	See macronutrients.
Margins:	Outermost edge of a leaf.
Meiosis:	The division of the chromosomes in the germ cells (pollen and ovules) of plants; causes each germ cell to contain one-half of the needed chromosomes for plant development.
Micronutrient:	Seven essential plant-food elements (zinc, copper,

190

	chlorine, manganese, iron, boron, and molybdenum) needed in only small amounts by plants.
Miniature African violet:	Plants that measure six or less inches in diameter at maturity.
Minor nutrients:	See micronutrients.
Miticide:	Any chemical that is used to kill mites.
Multicolored blossom:	Any blossom displaying two or more distinct colors.
Multicrown:	More than one crown per plant; frequently occurs whens suckers are not removed from an older plant.
Mutant:	Plants that have developed new features not seen in the parent plants: these changes occur naturally or can be chemically induced.
Natural lighting:	Any sunlight shining on the plants.
Neutral pH:	Scientific measurement used to explain a soil that is neither acid nor alkaline. When this situation occurs there is an equal amount of acid and alkaline forming chemicals present in the soil.
Nutrients:	Any of the sixteen plant foods needed by plants to sustain their growth.
Organic material:	Dead plants which have not yet begun to decompose; individual plant parts are distinguishable. Includes materials such as peanut hills, crushed corncobs, and peat.
Organic matter:	See humus.
Ovary:	The base of the pistil (female portion of a flower) where the seeds are formed.
Pasteurization:	Purification process used to rid special soil preparations of unwanted pests, such as insects, diseases, nematodes, and so on.
Peduncle:	The stalk arising from the crown of the plant, bearing a single blossom or a cluster of blossoms.
Petal:	Individual unit of a flower; in African violets a single blossom has five petals or units.
Peticel:	The stem that is attached to each blossom; branches off the main stalk (peduncle) to the blossoms.
Petiole:	The stem attached to each leaf.
pH:	Scientific measurement used to determine if the soil or any other substance is acid or alkaline. A pH number below 7 is acid, and above it is alkaline.
Phosphorylases:	Enzymes used as catalysis in chemical reactions occurring in individual plant cells.
Photochemical reaction:	The response obtained when light strikes specific chemical compounds in a plant's cells; photosynthesis is the best example of this phenomenon occurring in plants.

191

Photonastic:	The opening and closing of flowers as a response to the amount of light to which they are exposed.
Photoperiodism:	The response of flowering in plants as affected by the length of daylight.
Photosynthesis:	Production of food in plants through a complex reaction involving light, water, and carbon dioxide.
Phytochrome:	A chemical produced in a plant, in the presence of light, that causes flower buds to begin forming.
Phytoillumination:	Using light to grow plants.
Pistil:	The female portion of a flower consisting of three distinct parts—the ovary, the style, and the stigma.
Plant food:	See nutrients.
Plantlets:	Small immature leaves of a plant just beginning to develop from a leaf cutting; usually considered to be less than two inches tall and still attached to the parent cutting.
Pollen:	Powdery grains found in the anthers of a flower. Each grain carries half of the genetic code needed for the creation of a new plant.
Pollinating:	Transfer of pollen from the anthers to the pistil of a flower.
Propagate:	To produce new plants either from seed (sexual propagation) or by leaf cuttings, divisions, or separations (vegetative propagation).
Rays:	Refers to light in general as it is shining from either natural light or artificial lights.
Recessive gene:	Hereditary unit on the chromosomes that determines the traits a plant will display. Both matched genes from the parent must have the recessive characteristic for the trait to occur in the offspring. Recessive genes are subordinate to dominant genes.
Rootball:	Root and soil mass formed when plants are grown in containers.
Rooting hormone:	Special powdery substance which induces faster root formation when placed on the petiole of a leaf cutting.
Rooting mixture:	Artificially prepared soil mixture that has excellent drainage and the ability to store large amounts of moisture to allow quicker rooting of leaf cuttings.
Rootlets:	Small roots that are just forming.
Root zone:	Area in the soil mixture where a plant's roots are growing.
Rosette of leaves:	A circular arrangement of the leaves formed as they radiate out in all directions over the edge of the container.
Secondary nutrients:	Refers to three of the major plant nutrients—calcium,

	magnesium, and sulfur—needed by plants for normal growth.
Seedling:	Young plants that have emerged from seeds and are just starting to develop.
Semidouble blossom:	Blossoms with more than five petals but less than ten. Often a tuff of extra petals occurs in the center of the blossom.
Semiminiature African violets:	Plants measuring six to eight inches in diameter at maturity.
Separation:	Splitting apart two or more individual plants whose roots and leaves have become intertwined due to being grown close together in the same container.
Sexual propagation:	To produce new plants from seed.
Shortday plants:	Plants that flower only when there are ten to twelve hours of light shining on them each day.
Single blossom:	Blossoms with five petals. Usually divided into two lobes—the upper consisting of two smaller petals, and the lower having three larger petals. Frequently referred to as a standard blossom.
Slips:	See cuttings.
Soft water:	Water that has gone through a special tank and has had the hard salts (iron, calcium, magnesium, etc.) removed and replaced with sodium.
Soilbed:	Mixture of soil in which plants are being grown.
Soil mixture:	Refers to soil that has been prepared by mixing different ingredients together to create a special mixture for growing plants.
Sport:	See mutant.
Stamen:	The male portion of a flower responsible for pollen formation; consists of two distinct parts—the filament and the anthers.
Standard African violet:	Plants that measure between eight to sixteen inches in diameter at maturity.
Sterilization:	See pasteurization.
Stigma:	The uppermost tip of the pistil sticking out from the center of the flower; the organ that receives the pollen.
Strawberry pot:	Specialized plant pots with several openings around the sides large enough to insert a plant's soilball; allows a large number of plants to be grown in a small area.
Style:	A projection of the plant, usually protruding up through the center of the flower. One of the three structures which compose the female portion (pistil) of the flower.
Succulent leaves:	Thicker than normal leaves; unusually high amount of

	moisture is present in them.
Sucker:	A side shoot that develops from the crown of an old plant. If allowed to grow, a multicrown plant will be produced.
Supremes:	See Amazons.
Trace nutrients:	See micronutrients.
Transpiration:	The loss of water, as a vapor, from plant leaves.
Two-toned blossom:	Blossoms that display two different shades of the same color—for example, deep purple and lavender.
Variegated:	Usually refers to plant foliage which shows a combination of two different colors. Green leaves with splotches of white is the most common example seen in the plant kingdom.
Variety:	A subdivision of plant species; always very similar to the original plant but displaying minor changes that modify the appearance.
Vascular bundles:	Threadlike structures in which water and food are distributed throughout the plant.
Vegetative propagation:	See propagation.
Visible color spectrum:	The various colors that can be seen by the human eye after the light has been passed through a prism or reflected from the surface of an object.
Wavelengths:	Refers to the undulating characteristics of light rays as they travel through space.
Wick:	Any threadlike material that is used to draw moisture from a water-filled container into the soil where a plant is growing.
Xanthophylls:	Yellow to orange pigments found in the cells of plants.

194

Index

196

Phytochrome, 147
Phytoillumination, 151
Plant breeders, 10, 12, 27-28, 33-34
Plant breeding, 12, 33-42; genes and chromosomes, 37, 38, 39, 40; pollination of flowers, 35; record keeping, 34; seed development, 36; variegated plants, 41, 42; when to pollinate, 35
Plant diseases. *See* Diseases
Plant Gro lights, 154
Plant lice. *See* Aphids
Plant Lite lights, 154
Plant nutrients: classification of, 69; forms absorbed by the plants, 73; purpose of each, 70-72; sixteen essential ones, 68, 69
Plant problems. *See* Pests; Physiological diseases; Diseases. *See also individual pests*
Plastic pots. *See* Pots
Poinsettia, 142
Pollination of blossoms: best time of the year, 35; how to, 21, 35, 104; signs of, 36; transfer of genes, 36, 37
Pollination of plants, 104
Potash, 79
Potassium, 69, 70, 72, 76, 79, 90
Pots: clay, 52, 93; cleaning of, 99; containers for germinating seed, 121; determination of size, 96-97; glazed (ceramic), 52, 95; metal, 95; plastic, 94, 95; selection of, 92; short pots ideal, 96; size affects watering schedule, 44, 46; sterilization, 99; strawberry, 31, 99; unusual, 92
Pot size, effect on flowering, 95-97
Potting, guidelines, 97-99. *See also* Double potting
Potting mixtures. *See* Soil mixtures
Powdery mildew. *See* Diseases
Propagation: division of crown, 116-17; fertilizing, 114; final cut important, 105-6; length of time for roots to develop, 108; miniature greenhouse for rooting, 113; mite control, 106; rooting containers for soil mixes, 110-11; rooting in soil mixtures, 108-11; rooting in water, 106-8; rooting mixture temperatures, 110-11; soil mixture for rooting, 109-10; transferring from rooting mixture to pots, 115-16; when to transfer to pot, 108; pollination of flowers, 104; from seed, 120-22; selection of leaf, 105; separation of crowns, 116, 118; under lights, 167; vegetative versus sexual, 103-4
Proteins, 69, 70

Quarantine, 123, 127, 130, 137

Rainwater, 47, 107
Red spider mite, 138-39

Repotting, 100-102
Root growth: clay pots promote, 93; determining health of plants, 88
Rooting hormone, 111-12
Royal Botanical Gardens of Germany, 9, 12, 28

'Sailor Boy,' 12
Saint Paul, Baron Walter von, 9, 28
Saintpaulia ionantha: pronunciation, 14; scientific naming of, 12, 13
Saintpaulia species, 10, 12; *S. brevipilosa,* 28; *S. confusa,* 28, 30; *S difficilis,* 28; *S. diplotricha* Number 6, 29; *S. diplotricha* Number 0, 29; *S. goetzeana,* 29, 31; *S. grandifolia* Number 299, 29; *S. grandifolia* Number 237, 29; *S. grotei,* 29; *S. inconspicua,* 29; *S. intermedia,* 30; *S. ionantha,* 28, 30; *S. magungensis,* variety minima and variety occidentalis, 30; *S. nitida,* 30; *S. orbicularis,* variety purpurea, 30; *S. pendula,* variety kizarae, 30; *S. pusilla,* 30; *S. rupicola,* 31; *S. shumensis,* 31; *S. teitensis,* 31; *S. tongwensis,* 31; *S. velutina,* 31; *S. amaniensis,* 31; *S. House of Amani,* 31; *S. Sigi Falls,* 31
Salt accumulation, on pots and soil, 49, 56, 78, 127
Salt damage, to roots, 78, 79, 90
Salt problems, 46, 49, 56, 127
Salt stress, overcoming, 49, 56, 79, 80
Sand, 64, 82, 87
Sawdust, 82
Scales (insects), 133, 134
Secondary nutrients, 69, 73
Seed: number per flower pod, 21, 24, 34; size, 36; viability, 37; watering techniques for germination, 121
Seed hulls, 82
Seeding: container for, 121; germination bed, 120
Seedlings: intermediate transplanting, 121-22; when to transfer to pots, 122
Seed pod maturation, 24, 36
Seeds, drying in pod before planting, 121
Semiminiature African violets, 20
Shipping, care of plants when received, 178
Short day plants, 147; asters (most varieties), 148; begonia, 148; Christmas cactus, 148; chrysanthemums, 148; cocklebur, 148; cockscomb, 148; corn, 148; cosmos, 148; forsythia, 148; globeamaranth, 148; goldenrod, 148; kalanchoe, 148; lamb's quarters, 148; marigold, 148; morning glory, 148; poinsettias, 148; ragweed, 148; salvia, 148; soybean, 148; true violets, 148; zinnia, 148
Sinningia, 10
Slips. *See* Propagation
Sodium, 47, 79

Soft water, 47
Soft water conditioners, 47
Soil mixtures: addition of plant food, 90, 91;
    effect on watering schedule, 44; Cornell
    University mix, 86; crumble test for good
    mix, 88; garden loam, 87; ideal pH range,
    83, 84; ingredients, 82; Purdue University
    mix, 86; purpose of, 82, 85; testing of, 88;
    various types, 85-87; ways to heat for rooting
    leaves and germinating seeds, 110-11
Soils: clay and silt, 86, 87; prepackaged, 88
Soil sterilization: chemical treatment, 89; heat
    treatment, 89, 90, 99
Sphagnum peat. See Peat moss
Sponge rubber, 82
Sport, 12, 25, 38; occurrence in plants, 38
Springtails, 133, 134
Standard African violets, 20
Suckers, 24-25, 31, 118, 119
Sulfur, 47, 69, 71
Supremes, 38

Table salt, 79
Temperature: affects watering schedule, 44;
    ideal range, 60, 61; problems caused by too
    high, 61; problems caused by too low, 61;
    range originally found growing, 60; reversing
    day and night, 62; vacation setting, 54
Tanzania, Africa, 9
Thrips, 133, 135
Top watering. See Watering
Trace nutrients, 69, 73
Transpiration, 25
True violets, features compared with African
    violets. See African violets

Urea, 79
Urea formaldehyde, 79

Usambara Mountains, origin of African violets,
    9, 10, 11
Usambara Vielchen, 12

Vacationing, care of plants, 53-55
Variegated plants, 26. See also Hybridization
Variegation, what causes it, 41-42
Vermiculite: for drainage, 121; rooting mixture
    ingredient, 109; soil mixture ingredient, 64,
    82, 86, 87
'Viking,' 12
Violaceae family. See True violets
Violets. See African violets and True violets
Vitamins, 69, 70

Water: carrier of plant nutrients, 44; essential
    to growth, 43-44; quality, 47; sources of, 47;
    temperature, 47, 48, 57-58
Watering: effects on fertilizing schedule,
    77-78; amount, 45, 46; bottom, 49, 50; caus-
    ing sour soil, 48-49; determining when to,
    44-45; environment affects scheduling of,
    44; with a fertilizer solution, 55, 56; pots'
    effect on, 52; rewetting dried soil, 51; time
    of day, 45; top, 48, 49; vacation, 53-55; wick,
    50, 51, 55
Waterlogged soils, 46, 51
Wendland, Hermann, 9, 12
Wet wilt, 127
White flies, 179
Windows: drafts, 62; locations for plants, 148-
    49; temperature variations, 61
Winter feeding, 76
Woods earth, 82

Xanthophyll pigment, 145

Zinc, 69, 72